PENGUIN BOOKS

ACING COLLEGE

Joshua Halberstam teaches ethics at New York University. He has also taught at The New School for Social Research and at Long Island University, where he was associate professor of philosophy. Dr. Halberstam has been a college professor for more than fifteen years and has won numerous teaching awards. Among his many publications in his field, Professor Halberstam is editor of *Virtues and Values* (Prentice-Hall), an introductory text in ethics. In addition to his teaching, Professor Halberstam is a consultant in corporate communications and writes scripts for film and television.

D1509032

Acing College

A Professor Tells Students How to Beat the System

Joshua Halberstam, Ph.D.

PENGUIN BOOKS

PENGUIN BOOKS
Published by the Penguin Group
Viking Penguin, a division of Penguin Books USA Inc.,
375 Hudson Street, New York, New York 10014, U.S.A.
Penguin Books Ltd, 27 Wrights Lane,
London W8 5TZ, England
Penguin Books Australia Ltd, Ringwood,
Victoria, Australia
Penguin Books Canada Ltd, 2801 John Street,
Markham, Ontario, Canada L3R 1B4
Penguin Books (N.Z.) Ltd, 182–190 Wairau Road,
Auckland 10, New Zealand

Penguin Books Ltd, Registered Offices:
Harmondsworth, Middlesex, England

First published in Penguin Books 1991

1 3 5 7 9 10 8 6 4 2

LIBRARY OF CONGRESS CATALOGING IN PUBLICATION DATA
Halberstam, Joshua, 1946–
Acing college: a professor tells students how to beat the system/
Joshua Halberstam.
p. cm.
ISBN 0 14 01.3998 2
1. College student orientation—United States.   2. Study, Method of.
I. Title.
LB2343.32.H35   1991
378.1'98—dc20   90-23405

Printed in the United States of America

Set in Century Expanded
Designed by Kathryn Parise

For my students:

past, present, and future

Preface

In my more than fifteen years of college teaching, I've seen hundreds of students with the same story. Though bright and conscientious, these students don't excel in their classes. Their problem is that they don't understand how the grading system really works. Some students figure this out on their own, some don't, and most understand part of the system but not all of it.

I decided to help. I would share the grading secrets of professors with students.

How do you get A's?

By studying. It helps, too, if you're smart. No surprise here—these are the obvious and correct answers—and this book offers advice on how to study and become smart. But studying and smarts are only part of the solution. They are what we call "necessary conditions"—you won't get good grades (at least not often) without some brains and lots of diligence. But these are not "sufficient conditions"— to ace college you'll need more. You will need to know how grades are determined and how your behavior contributes to that grading process. This book aims at explaining this crucial subjective part of the grading game too.

Although *Acing College* is based on my own experience as a college professor, I made sure to discuss it in detail with many of my colleagues in the profession. Each, as expected, had his or her own war story and favorite piece of advice; some preferred that I emphasize certain points that others would ignore entirely. But what I found most surprising—and comforting in its way—was the consensus about the validity of this material. College grading, it turns out, is pretty much the same all over.

Much of what you read here will seem obvious. I hope so; if it's all new to you, you're in big trouble. But let me assure you, too, that every suggestion included here is repeatedly violated by students, even at the better universities.

Restating the obvious has its benefits: part of learning is having your beliefs confirmed. But what some find obvious, others find surprising, and I suspect everyone will find something new and unexpected in these suggestions.

I also want to remind you that what follows are guidelines, not inviolable rules. Your professor might have her own idiosyncratic way of devising exams and grading, and what works for most might not work for you. You will have to determine your own best approach to your classes. The recommendations you find here will help you get started.

So here's the deal. I'll tell you about the hidden process of grading: the best way to study for exams, how to do well on short-answer tests, what professors look for on essays and term papers—what they *really* look for, not just what they say they look for. I'll tell you where to sit, what classroom behavior impresses professors and what turns them off, whether to show up for office hours, the dumbest way to cheat, which teachers to take and which to avoid, and even how to fake it on exams in emergencies . . . and lots more.

And your part of the deal? You have to read these tips as they are intended—*as an addition to your studies, not a replacement for them*. Without hard work, these recommendations are useless.

You also have to agree to think about the place of grades in your life. I don't have to convince you that good grades are important not only to your future but to your present sense of accomplishment as well. Grades are the nearest thing to an objective measure of your academic success in college. On the basis of your grades you are the recipient of honors or placed on probation, accepted or rejected by the graduate school of your choice, hired or passed over by your first potential employer.

What I may have to convince you of is that grades are subsidiary to your other educational goals. In fact, as we'll see later on, an obsessive concern with grades is an obstacle to getting good grades. You need to put grades in their proper perspective. That means seeing your self-worth in your accomplishments, not your transcript.

If you agree, we can make that transcript look good. Here's how. . . .

Acknowledgments

First thanks go to my colleagues and friends who assuaged my worries about sharing professorial secrets with students. Their encouragement was unabated. I thank them, too, for sharing with me their own classroom experiences and for their moral support.

An idea does not a book make. But Agnes Birnbaum does. She saw an article I had published on professors and students, recognized a book lurking there, and agented it into life. I thank her for her intuition, graciousness, and steady guidance.

A big thanks, too, to Roger Devine, my editor at Penguin. Meticulous and excellent editor that he is, Roger quickly understood what I wanted to say and helped me say it better.

And thanks, as always, to my wife, Yocheved Cohen, for her right-on recommendations and Promethean patience.

Contents

1

You and Your Professor

If you can't do, teach. If you can't teach, teach phys-ed.

What qualities should I look for in choosing my professors?

Is it worth the trouble of sitting in on a class of a professor I'm thinking of taking next term?

Should I make a point of seeing my professor during his office hours? I have nothing to talk about—but will it help my grade?

What's the difference between a lecturer, an assistant professor, and an associate professor? Is one more likely than the other to give higher grades?

In July of 1967, Dr. Harvey Martin Friedman was appointed a professor of mathematics at Stanford University. He was eighteen years old. In 1913 Joel Hildebrand became a professor. Sixty-eight years later, in 1981, he published his 275th paper. He was ninety-nine years old and still teaching!

Your professor can be very young or very old. He is a respected scholar or someone who hasn't read a book in his field in fifteen years. She is energetic, enthusiastic, interested in students, or a distant bore. Some professors are dynamic and inspiring . . . others, simply dreadful.

Professors determine the success of your class and also your grades, so it makes sense to choose your professors carefully. Yet many students have no idea how to go about selecting their teachers, and even less of an idea how to act toward them once they do enroll in their classes. The result? Lower grades. This need not happen to you.

CAN TEACHERS TEACH?

The Bad News: Most Professors Are Poor Teachers

You've seen the movies. You've watched dashing teachers inspire novice students to heights of cerebral delirium. You've cheered as intellectually courageous, super-sensitive and brilliant professors battle for the hearts and minds of their eager undergraduates.

Welcome to reality. If you want to avoid disappointments later on, you need realistic expectations now. One thing you shouldn't expect is a battery of professors who resemble those thrilling creations of the media. You who have already spent some time in college know this. The rest of you will learn the stark truth soon enough.

Most college professors are lousy teachers. Of course, of course, many college professors are also wonderful teachers. Nevertheless, when it comes to teaching ability, your average college professor is about average—or worse.

To understand why this is so, you need to recognize one

important fact about the college faculty system: **college professors are not rewarded by their employers for good teaching.**

A popular professor who attracts a hundred students to his class does not get paid more than the professor who has to bribe students to take his class. The superior teacher doesn't get a lighter teaching load, more vacation, or a bigger bonus at Christmas. The rewards for good teaching are substantial, but they are the rewards of personal satisfaction, not institutional compensation. Good teaching doesn't "pay" (professionally, that is).

When you consider why professors teach in college, it isn't surprising that so many of them lack teaching skills. They enter this line of work because they care about their subjects, not because they care about teaching. Their professional rewards are for excellence in publishing, not excellence in instruction. For many professors, teaching is a side pursuit and a drag, and it becomes more of a drag as the years march on.

Some of your professors teach because it's a secure way to make a living. Obviously, don't look to this group for your dazzling professor.

(Most professors, by the way, don't even make it as scholars. According to a recent survey reported in the *Wall Street Journal*, 60 percent of all college faculty have never written or edited a book and a third have never published a single article.)

Now for the Really Bad News: Teaching Assistants

You might consider yourself lucky having a professor who can't teach. More and more often, your teacher will be a graduate student who can't teach.

Universities are increasingly hiring teaching assistants,

called T.A.s, to teach classes. This is especially the case in larger universities; at Yale, for example, 25 percent of all undergraduate classes are taught by teaching assistants. Which classes? T.A.s typically teach introductory courses—courses that hot-shot, established professors would rather not teach. Unfortunately, these are the classes in which good teaching is essential.

Most T.A.s are even worse teachers than college professors. T.A.s are hired because they are a source of cheap labor. They are overworked and don't receive respect from their students. They are more worried about their own graduate courses than about your course. T.A.s are not a happy crew.

A growing number of these graduate assistants are foreign students with poor English skills. Foreign graduate students are especially prominent in science, math, and economics departments (why such a high percentage of graduate students in these subjects is foreign is a different, sad story about American education). These graduate assistants teach a substantial portion of the math and science undergraduate classes—the classes that require the highest degree of explanatory skill.

The Good News: Bad Teaching Is Not So Bad

Most college learning takes place outside of the classroom. Your grades are determined, for the most part, on your writing and research abilities, your understanding of the textbook, your study and test-taking skills, and other factors that don't directly depend on your professor's teaching ability. Sure it helps if you have a teacher who can teach well, but you can get an A even with the worst of the lot. If your professor is boring, you'll have to work a little harder at paying attention, and if he doesn't elucidate the material, you'll have to study more diligently. You can manage.

But why settle for a second-rate instructor when you can choose a first-rate instructor? The trick is knowing what to look for.

YOUR PROFESSOR *IS* THE COURSE

Sometimes you must take a class at a specific time, and only one professor is teaching it, but usually you can choose the professor you want. **In choosing the professor, you also choose the course.**

American History 11.2 as taught by Professor Wishwash is not the same American History 11.2 as taught by Professor Cumsicumsa. Forget what the catalogue says.* Even if two professors offer similar syllabi, they are teaching different classes. Science and mathematics courses depend less on who teaches them, but even in these classes, *what* is taught depends on *how* it's taught.

Professor Shopping: The Criteria

When choosing your teacher, you want to know about three essential qualities:

- Is the professor interesting?
- Is the professor fair?
- Is the professor available?

---

* Course descriptions have little to do with the course content and a lot to do with marketing. Departments make up names and blurbs for courses on the basis of what will sell with students—much as marketers do with cereals and soaps.

Is the professor interesting?

This is perhaps the most important feature of all. If your teacher is boring, you'll be bored, and if you're bored, you won't do your work, and if you don't do your work, you won't learn, and if you don't learn, you won't do well in the course. It's that simple. You might think that because the course material seems easy, the class is an easy A, but it doesn't work that way. A dull, easy course quickly becomes a dull, hard course. You soon begin to hate coming to class and start cutting; when you are there, you're there only in body, not in mind.

You're looking for a professor whose enthusiasm will make *you* enthusiastic about the subject. To insure an A in any class, you have to care about the subject matter.

Is the professor fair?

You want a professor with a reputation for giving assignments and exams that accurately test student achievements—one who is impartial and fair.

What about seeking out the "high graders"? Don't bother; it's a waste of time.

Of course, you should stay away from the professor who gives only one A per decade, or decides grades on the basis of the student's initials. You don't want a teacher who is fickle or a sadist.

But most professors mark within the same range. Differences occur in the borderlines: one teacher will lean toward the C+, another toward the B−, but almost all professors aim for a balanced distribution of grades. They have to: if they mark too high, they lose the respect of their colleagues, while if they mark too low, they won't have any students to grade.

The proper attitude: I'll do my job and assume my teacher will do hers.

Is the professor available?

"Available" here means available for consultation. (We'll get to the other kind of "available" later.) Yes, even you, brilliant student that you are, might hit a snag in your study. You, young Einstein, might lose your way with your paper and appreciate your professor's clarification. Will he be there for you?

"Being there" is primarily a matter of attitude. Many professors rush out of the room as soon as the class is over. You chase your professor down the stairs, finally catch up with him, and breathlessly ask him your question. He stops for a nanosecond, blurts out a yes or no, and is off faster than that rabbit on his way to the tea party. You feel as if you are imposing. You aren't—answering students' questions is part of a teacher's job.

A professor who insists on leaving right after class is a professor you can do without. In fact, you want a professor who *encourages* your questions and comments.

Other telltale signs of second-rate professors:

- Inferior professors regurgitate the textbook. You end up paying lots of money to have someone read to you.
- Inferior teachers rely on notes they made twenty years ago. The material is stale, and so are they.
- Inferior teachers come to class unprepared so they resort to:

  - Bull sessions. These are usually dominated by the biggest mouth in the class. The professor doesn't care as long as it eats up the clock. You have far more enlightening conversations at the coffee shop.

- Audio-visual aids/films. Professors maintain that movies "engage" the student and that showing films to a class is an "effective, contemporary method of transmitting information." Sure, movies sometimes succeed as a pedagogical tool—especially in film classes. But professors often resort to audio-visual devices because they're too lazy to teach the class. So watch out for professors who devote more than a few of their classes to the screen.
- Inferior teachers are jargon addicts. They hide behind their professional buzzwords and make no concerted effort to explain what they say.
- Inferior teachers sit in their chairs; better teachers sit on their desks or don't sit at all.

PROFESSOR SHOPPING:
THE PROCESS

Let's observe Wendy as she goes about deciding who to take for her English Lit. class. She needs this particular class and knows what she wants in a professor. Professor Allison Wonderland is teaching the class that fits into her schedule. How does Wendy find out if ol' Dr. Wonderland has what it takes?

Other Students

The first thing Wendy should do is ask other students about the professor. It turns out that Wendy's roommate had once taken a class with Professor Wonderland.

"Is she any good?" Wendy asks.

"Good?" the roommate exclaims. "Good? You've got to be kidding. The woman is the worst. Her tests are so hard you couldn't crack them with a sledgehammer. She thinks this is Princeton's Institute for Advanced Studies or something. Forget it."

Wendy inquires what grade her roommate received in the class. "She flunked me," her roommate answers weakly.

Does Wendy also know that her roommate flunked six classes, and that her poor academic performance has put her on probation? This roommate thinks all her teachers are too difficult and is hardly a reliable judge of professors.

By the same token, Wendy shouldn't expect much help from Jennifer, who never gets anything less than an A. Every class is a breeze for her but maybe not for Wendy.

Talk to students but watch out for hasty generalizations (the fallacy of generalizing from too small or unusual a sample). Talk to a range of students: the good, the bad, and the ugly.

Other Members of the Department

Should Wendy talk to other members of Professor Wonderland's department? No. First of all, professors are unlikely to give her a straight answer about their colleague. It's unprofessional and uncomfortable, too. Think of the consequences if a professor finds out one of her colleagues is bad-mouthing her.

Second, even if Wendy does get a colleague to answer her questions about Professor Wonderland, what she hears is biased. Professors are prone to judge their colleagues on the quality of their writing, their politics, their private lives, and other factors that have little to do with you as a student. Students who sit in classes are in a much better position to judge a professor's teaching ability than other professors.

You can ask a professor with whom you have a close relationship whether it's advisable to take a class with Professor So-and-so. But phrase the question in such a way that your professor-friend can make a gesture that hints at the answer.

Should You Sit In on the Professor's Class?

Wendy can learn a whole lot about Wonderland's teaching style by auditing her class. She will learn how Professor Wonderland relates to her class, and how the class relates to her.

Auditing a class isn't always a realistic option. You probably have a class at the same time that professor teaches. More important, many professors don't want you to sit in; visitors make them feel uncomfortable. It's one thing if you're auditing because you're interested in the subject matter, but it's something else if you're there to do an evaluation. Who likes to be judged?

In no case should you sit in without permission. The classroom is the professor's turf and she has the prerogative to forbid guests. You're running some risk if you barge in. The professor might not object now, but she might remember your brashness next term when you're registered in her class, and this certainly won't help your grade. Always ask beforehand if it's all right to visit a class.

Visit the Bookstore

Wendy would do well to visit the bookstore. Books are hardly the whole story—teaching ability is far more important—but they give you a solid clue about the upcoming class.

Professors are asked to submit booklists at least a month before the beginning of the term. They are notorious for being late, but most manage to submit their lists before classes begin. Check out the reading list or the books themselves, if they are in.

The Syllabus

Let's assume that Wendy has settled on her professor and is ready for the first day of class. She awaits her syllabus to find out what to expect from the class.

Most professors hand out a syllabus at the first class. If Professor Wonderland doesn't distribute a syllabus, Wendy can draw one of two conclusions: either the professor is disorganized and hasn't figured out what she wants to do, or she's a free spirit who doesn't want to saddle the class with a rigid schedule. Wendy will find out soon enough which is the case.

When you're handed a syllabus, look at it carefully.

A long and very exact syllabus indicates an exacting grader. Your professor is probably a stickler for detail and rules (you can bet, for example, that he or she won't appreciate any late papers). If the syllabus contains specific information about how grades are computed, that's exactly how your grade will be computed.

Most syllabi are much looser game plans, and during the first few weeks you'll find out how much of that plan actually comes into play.

The syllabus is a crucial tip-off. If the course seems exceedingly dull or incredibly difficult, the time to bail out is sooner rather than later.

But give yourself some time to see if the syllabus is a bluff. Some professors prepare these intricate syllabi and then never look at them again. This is particularly true of the "recommended readings." A long list of such readings looks impressive, but your professor probably doesn't actually expect you to read these books; in fact, he probably hasn't read half of them himself.

PROFESSORS AND STATUS: WHAT YOU NEED TO KNOW

Too often, students judge their teachers on the basis of their ranking, professional status or age. Most students (and most everyone else too) are confused about the ranking system and how it affects their grades.

How Professors Are Ranked

College teachers have rankings, and titles that correspond to these rankings. The lowest level is instructor, the next higher level is lecturer, then assistant professor, followed by associate professor, and finally full professor. (Some universities dispense with the categories of instructors and lecturers and hire their junior faculty as assistant professors.) These rankings are formal titles and have little to do with real power or scholarly achievement. To move up the academic ladder, you generally need to do some publishing and put in some time in committee work. The requirements differ from college to college. But what counts most is survival. Typically, one gets promoted to the next higher rank as a reward for enduring long enough.

What are the advantages of moving up in the ranks? Very few. With each promotion, you get a little bit more money—but let me stress the "little bit" part: college teachers get paid little to begin with, so these increments are insignificant. Higher rankings also fetch a little more prestige. Your professor is addressed by her full title when interviewed on the radio: for example, Sharon Wormbook, associate professor of English. The higher the rank, the more "established" the professor.

And what do these rankings mean to *you*, the student? Not much. We noted that the main factor in moving up the ranking ladder is seniority. But one of the things that counts *least* in professorial ranking is teaching ability. Here's the main point: **your teacher's professorial rank is no guide whatsoever to his or her teaching ability.**

The Administration

Ever notice how many people on campus are called dean? Dean This, Dean That. These deans are part of what is called the college administration. Although some administrators teach, and most have taught, they are not part of the teaching faculty. In fact, faculty and administration often don't get along at all.

The college president is the big chief. You'll see him or her at graduations and at special events. Most colleges also have an array of vice presidents who are responsible for various functions, such as finance and planning. The ones you might have something to do with are the vice president for academic affairs (whose responsibilities include curriculum and faculty appointees) and the vice president for student affairs (whose domain encompasses campus housing and extracurricular activities). However, chances are that in the course of your four years in college you won't speak more than two sentences to any vice president.

Deans are the next lower level in the administration hierarchy. You might have a Business Dean or a Dean of

Arts and Sciences. If you have a problem with a professor that a department chairperson can't handle, you have to take it up with the appropriate dean. In most colleges you only meet deans when you get awards or are in big trouble.

What Is Tenure?

Tenure is another term you've heard but might not understand. Generally, after five to seven years of teaching at a college, professors are "up for tenure." Tenure means assured job security. To get fired after receiving tenure, a professor would have to do something outrageous—perhaps shoot a student who contradicted the professor in class. (And even then, the professor might come up with a defensible argument.) A mix of factors enters into a tenure decision: a bit of merit (publishing and committee work), a dash of timing (a thriving economy and thriving student enrollment), and a lot of politics (the candidate is liked by his colleagues and the college administration).

The original reason for tenure was to protect teachers from getting fired because of their political views; in the classroom the professor is supposed to have the freedom to expound any view he advocates. These days, the need for this protection still occasionally arises, but for the most part tenure has become, according to its critics, little more than a job cushion.

Tenured professors don't have to prove anything anymore, and they don't have to produce. Some professors, particularly at better schools, continue to work in their field even after they get tenure. But for many professors, tenure provides the security to devote their time and energies to other interests and spells the end of their scholarly life. What does all this mean in terms of choosing your professor? Should you care if your teacher is tenured? The short answer is: no. The longer answer is: probably not.

The one case where tenure might make a direct difference to you is when your teacher is a younger professor up for tenure in the next year or two. These "tenure track" professors are on exceptionally good behavior, especially as they get closer to the time for their tenure decision. They will make sure to publish as much as they can, meet their committee assignments, and teach conscientiously. Sometimes having an overly conscientious teacher can work against you—such professors are maddeningly meticulous.

Staff

Examine your course bulletin. Most courses have a professor's name listed alongside the hours but many courses simply say "staff." Who is this Ms. Staff who teaches so many classes?

Some of the staff are the T.A.s we discussed earlier. The rest are part-time faculty. In fact, 25 percent of all faculty in four-year colleges is part-time.

Part-time or adjunct faculty are, like T.A.s, another source of cheap labor for the university. They get paid per course at a rate far less than full timers. And they do not receive employee benefits. Many are unhappy and frustrated at not having full-time positions, while others have non-academic jobs and teach because they like teaching. A sizable portion of adjuncts teach because they want the academic address, for personal or business reasons.

Part-time faculty are a motley crew. They vary right across the board in scholarship and teaching ability.

Although you may prefer to take classes with full-time teachers, your schedule might demand that you take classes with part timers as well. It's a good idea to enroll in classes taught by those adjunct professors who have a history at the university and a track record you can rely on; some part-timers are like travelling salesmen who show up one day and disappear the next. You want a professor who will deal with problems that arise: concluding an incomplete, checking on a mistaken grade, getting a letter of recommendation, etc.

Other professors listed as staff are visiting professors. "Visitors" are usually selected because of their esteem. This is a wonderful opportunity to study with someone with a national reputation in his field. A note of caution, however: this reputation is based on the visiting professor's scholarship, not his teaching ability. If you are a freshman, it makes little difference which journal featured the person's work. Good teaching is a bigger concern.

Does Your Professor's Age Make a Difference?

There are no hard and fast correlations between a professor's age and teaching ability or grading tendencies, but some patterns are worth noting. Junior professors tend to exude more energy—they're younger, more eager, more concerned with making a name in their field. *But many of the toughest graders are younger professors.* Fresh out of graduate school, starting-out professors relish the other side of the desk and make their students suffer for all the horrible hours they recently spent working toward their degrees. They need reminding that they shouldn't expect from their freshmen class what their Ph.D. advisors expected from them.

What about the older professor? Colleges did a great deal of hiring in the sixties, so expect an increasing population of older professors in the nineties and beyond. Some older professors are dynamic and have distinguished careers as outstanding teachers, while others fell asleep a decade ago and haven't awoken. Recently, a student complained to me about her aged teacher who delivered the same lecture three times in a row! Often, these semi-senile professors are easy graders; they have nothing more to prove and can afford generosity. On the other hand, you won't learn very much from them.

DEALING WITH YOUR PROFESSOR

How Do I Address My College Teacher?

"Hey Teach!" isn't the right answer. A few professors—maybe six in the entire country—will think you're chummy. Everyone else will think you're an obnoxious adolescent. Don't get cutesy.

First names? Back in the sixties, many professors were delighted when their students called them by their first names. Back then, titles were seen as part of the evil authoritarian establishment. Those days are gone. The students of the sixties are now your professors and they enjoy their titles.

Here's the rule: unless you've been told specifically and unmistakably otherwise, **do not call your professor by his or her first name**.

Does this seem obvious? I'd think so, too, were it not for all those students who slap me on the back and ask, "How's it going, Joshua?" Perhaps it's unfair that professors call you by your first name but you don't call them by their first names, but fairness isn't the issue here, grades are. If you don't want to risk a lower grade, address your teacher by the proper title.

Which title? "Your Lordship" is overdoing it, and "Your

Majesty" is already taken. If your teacher has a Ph.D., the title "doctor" will do fine. Ph.D., by the way, stands for Doctor of Philosophy (or *Philosophiae Doctor*, if you want to get persnickety). In these times of scarce teaching jobs, particularly in the humanities and social sciences, most of your teachers will have doctorates, and some of these Ph.D.s care a great deal that you recognize their academic achievement. Take note: this sensitivity is especially common with junior faculty who have recently received their degrees.

For those of your teachers who do not have doctorates (teaching assistants, for example), the title "doctor" is inappropriate. If you aren't sure whether or not your instructor has a doctorate, play it safe by addressing him as "professor."

Professor Who? Professor Szyszmaniac, That's Who

Learn to pronounce your teacher's name correctly. And take pains to spell it correctly, too. Even if it's Szyszmaniac. Everyone notices when his name is misspelled. Misspell your professor's name and he will notice your carelessness—notice, that is, that you care less than you should. You've failed to verify something easily verified, and that starts your paper or exam on the wrong foot. This might seem trivial, but little defects such as these can make the difference between a good grade and the A.

Office Hours

During the first few classes, your professor will also announce her office hours. Pay attention.

The official reason for office hours is to provide students

with the opportunity to ask questions or make comments inappropriate in the classroom. You may be too shy to ask for help in public, or your question may be complicated and would take up too much class time. Perhaps you have a personal problem that requires discussion in private. So much for official reasons—what's the reality?

In general, office hours are frauds. The majority of professors don't show up for their office hours and neither do their students. Instructors list hours to make their chairpersons and deans happy, and then everyone ignores the whole thing. A few professors are in their offices all the time, working away. Other professors never come in at all. Neither case has anything to do with the required office hours.

If you want to see your professor, don't rely on scheduled hours. Make an appointment.

Use the appointment wisely: don't visit your professor just to "shoot the breeze." Some professors will appreciate the wind, but most won't. Even those professors who have nothing better to do like to believe they do—and like you to believe they do.

Visit your professor if you are having trouble with the class material and need further explanation. There's a fine line here: your professor doesn't want to be your tutor and you won't present yourself as an A student if you repeatedly come for tutorial help.

Visit your professor, too, if you get seriously interested in the subject. You learn most from a professor when he's off his classroom pedestal and relaxing in his chair. Gossip about the thinkers in the field, listen to your professor's pet theories, find out what else to read. You will not only learn a lot, you will also elevate yourself from the ordinary student. But remember, you can't fake that interest; either you care about the subject or you don't.

Don't Plead for Grades

One of my students attached a note to the end of her final exam that went something like this:

> Dear Professor Halberstam,
>   Please see your way to give me at least a B+ for this class. If I receive anything less, my index will drop below a B average and my father will take away my horse. Horse-riding is an essential part of my life (I'm on the equestrian team). Without my horse my social life will collapse. My very sanity depends on a good grade, so please. . . . P.S. I loved your class.

Here was my choice: Either I give her a B+ or I'm to blame if she were committed to an insane asylum. (She got the C she deserved and remained perfectly sane.)

Pleading for grades is a waste of time at best and counter-productive at worst.

I'm still amazed at how students shamelessly ask for a higher grade. "I *need* the A to maintain a scholarship," they beseech, or "I *must have* the C to avoid being placed on probation," they whimper. Do these students believe that whining helps?

The student is not claiming that she *merits* a higher grade but only that she *needs* the higher grade. Appeals to pity are an admission that you don't deserve a higher grade on the basis of your work. But it is merit—and nothing else—that should determine your grade.

Suppose you believe you do deserve a higher grade? Suppose you think your grade is unfair?

Arguing with your professor is like arguing an umpire's call: you can't win. This is especially true when you are arguing about your grade on an essay or paper. Grading here is partly subjective and the professor can, and usually will, insist on the correctness of his judgment. You, on the other hand, come off as petty and spoiled; you'll attract his ire, not his sympathy. So pleading a midterm grade is risky.

The one occasion where you should *insist* on reviewing your grade is when the professor has miscalculated your points or made some other blatant, careless error. Otherwise, take what you get.

Letters of Recommendation

Remember those "three greatest lies"? One was "Your check is in the mail." I can't remember the second, and the third I can't print.

Well, here's a candidate for the fourth-biggest lie: letters of recommendation.

When you apply to graduate school or for jobs, you'll hunt for teachers to write wonderful things about you in letters of recommendation.

Most professors will write them for you. They'll write that you're conscientious, responsible, made a significant contribution to the class, and then add a few other vacuous comments.

Universities and professional schools realize how little these letters reflect reality. They've learned how to translate: "Tracey is a conscientious, first-rate student" means that Tracey is okay; "Tracey is a good student" means she's the pits.

Schools also realize how lazy professors are when it comes to writing recommendations, so they give them boxes to fill out: "Mark the box that best characterizes the student: superior, above average, average, below average." Next, they are given a list of character traits to grade accordingly. Dutifully, the professor checks off the boxes.

It doesn't matter if he doesn't remember you. Writing letters of recommendation is like filling out insurance forms; it's part of the job.

Needless to say, these prefab recommendations aren't going to get you into Harvard graduate school. If you want a worthwhile letter of recommendation:

- Ask for letters only from professors who gave you an A in their class. If you received a lower grade, your teacher can't write that you're extra special.
- Ask teachers you had more than once. The forms ask the professor to say how long he has known the applicant, and the longer the better. In addition, if you've taken more than one class with a professor, he will feel more comfortable praising you.
- Ask your professor what he will write. He won't tell you precisely, but you can get a good idea. If he tells you that in all honesty he'll write only a fair recommendation on your behalf—you're a decent, competent student (but no better)—forget it. A mediocre recommendation is usually worse than no recommendation. Ask someone else.
- Don't insist on reading the letter of recommendation. It inhibits the writer. If you want your professor to lie about you and say complimentary things, let him lie in private.

Getting Personal

"Hey, is Professor Studman married?" "Do you think he does drugs?" "I hear Professor Glitter married a lot of money." "What do you think she's like at parties?"

Students are naturally curious about their professors and exhibit their curiosity in various ways. Some of those ways aren't very smart—especially if you care about your grades.

Do not discuss your professor's private life in class.

Unless your professor brings it up for discussion, do not refer to his life, wife, or strife. Your professor's personal history is off-limits in the classroom. If you're privy to juicy information about your teacher, do all your whispering before he or she enters the room. Professors are sensitive about their privacy.

Getting Really Personal

Romantic stirrings between professors and students are common in college. That's not surprising; an environment of adult males and adult females usually gives rise to romantic stirrings. These romances go both ways—professors are attracted to students and vice versa—but problems lurk about.

Scenario number one. Your professor comes on to you, but he reminds you of the Hunchback of Notre Dame. You are very definitely not interested. What to do?

First, make it clear that you don't want to play. You can make your aversion very plain and when you do, your professor will almost always back off. Not only is it obnoxious to persist when rejected, it's professionally stupid.

What if your professor doesn't desist with his advances? Worse still, suppose your professor hints that your grade depends on your sexual favors? This level of crudity is extremely rare—but if it happens, the matter is very serious, and you should treat it seriously. First, talk to your professor and make your annoyance very clear. If he or she continues to solicit your favors, mention it to the department chairperson. Bring it to even higher authorities if it still isn't resolved.

But what if you enjoy your professor's flirtation? Or, suppose you're the one who initiates the flirting, you're the one who's infatuated?

Sexual intimacies between professors and students are delicate affairs; when they go sour, both professor and student can get seriously hurt. Both believe they are discreet and fully capable of separating the personal relationship from the professional one. But it's never that simple. The student is self-conscious in the classroom and insecure about his performance while the professor struggles to maintain objectivity when grading the student who shares her bed.

Ah, but romance has a way of defying the most complicated of circumstances, does it not? What if the two of you are helplessly in love? Your professor lingers in your imagination hours after the class is over. You want to stay away, but you are propelled to each other. What then?

Okay, Mr. or Ms. Starry-eyed. These passionate longings are not infrequent and many professors are married to their former students. Far be it from me to argue against amour. But do control your temptation until the term is over and thereby avoid a possible conflict of interest. Even if your professor cannot, surely *you* can manage that much restraint.

Develop a Mentor

Someday, somewhere in the middle of your college career, you may run into a professor who makes a real difference in your life. This professor inspires you, challenges you to think in ways you've never thought before. This is the professor who gets you to believe in yourself, who convinces you that you have what it takes to succeed. Don't turn away from this professor—this situation presents a rare opportunity.

Take additional courses with this professor. Talk to him. Let him guide your intellectual development. This isn't an imposition; to the contrary, professors are delighted to discover enthusiastic students.

When one of your teachers is transformed into a mentor, you enter a very special and enriching relationship. As with other serious associations, the mentor–student relationship requires a commitment on both sides. And like other enduring personal connections, this one, too, will have its rocky patches and tensions. It will also have its moments of great personal satisfaction.

Your mentor will become the most rewarding educational investment of your life. Not many college students ever get this intellectually close to a professor, and if you do, you are truly fortunate.

Class in the Classroom

> One always speaks badly when one has nothing
> to say.
>
> —VOLTAIRE

Does attendance really count?

What's the best place to sit in the classroom?

Does class participation really matter?

The dos and don'ts of classroom behavior

Kid knocks on my office door. He looks vaguely familiar. "My name is Scott," he says. "I'm in your logic class." Yes, that's why I recognize him; he's the fellow who showed up a couple of times at the beginning of the semester. Sat in the back, I think.

"So where have you been all term?" I ask with genuine curiosity. "Well," the student fumbles, "I'm taking this tough course in organic chemistry, and well, uh, like I got this lazy attitude, I admit. Anyway, I'd like an extension on my term paper deadline. And would you reconsider my midterm grade?"

I listen, but I don't listen sympathetically. I'm certainly not inclined to reward this student for his lack of interest in my class. It's not a matter of an official policy—I don't take attendance. But I don't have to do favors either, and I rarely do for students who don't show up to class.

"The most important thing in life is showing up," says Woody Allen. That's true, too, with regard to your classes.

In this chapter we'll discuss how to make the most of your time when you're in class. But these guidelines are useful only if you're there to use them.

SHOWING UP

On any given school day, you could probably think of seven thousand more fun things to do than go to class. One compelling alternative is to just stay in bed. In fact, staying in bed will loom as one of the greatest temptations of college life.

I take it for granted that if you aren't thoroughly dull or irrecovably compulsive, you will miss class on occasion. What does it take for you to decide "forget it, I'll skip class"? A blah, rainy day? A gorgeous, sunny day? Students' cutting patterns get fixed pretty early in their college career. The question is not whether you will miss class, but how often.

Some professors include attendance as part of their course requirements. These professors usually carry out their threat. The more stringent ones will even fail the A student who has accrued too many absences. Unfair? I agree. In fact, I find this outrageous. With few exceptions (labs, for example), I favor abolishing all attendance requirements. College students are adults and should decide for themselves whether or not they want to come to class. If you never show up, you risk flunking your tests—but that's *your* problem. On the other hand, if you never show up and get A's on your exams, you should receive an A for the course.

Why do professors require attendance? Many will tell you it's because students need to attend their lectures to understand the material. And they quickly emphasize the need for an "attendance requirement" for those students who lack sufficient discipline to show up regularly without this externally imposed threat.

Hogwash. Professors require attendance, in most cases, because they are insecure. They're afraid that if they don't take attendance, no one will show up—and they're usually right. Not surprisingly, it's most often the dull teachers who force their students to suffer through their dreary lectures.

What can you do about these attendance requirements? Nothing. Maybe you can do something later when you become the college president, but until then, if you have an attendance requirement, show up. You have no choice.

But even if you don't have an attendance requirement, it's important to show up regularly.

If you want to ace your classes, cut out cutting. You might think your case is different. But I can only assure you of what all my colleagues and I see: A students show up to class regularly, and F students don't. Here's why.

Objectively

You'll learn more. Nothing beats being there. When you study without having been to class, you're learning the material for the first time. When you study after you've been to class, you're reviewing. What a difference!

You learn what the professor considers essential. Professors test you on what they consider important. What did the professor put on the blackboard? What did he emphasize? What did he repeat?

You can't get this information from another student's notes, or even a tape recording. You need to observe first-hand your professor's delivery: you need to know not only *what* was said but *how* it was said.

Subjectively

In the subjective realm of grading, attendance always counts. Professors respond positively toward students who come to class regularly. Repeated absences will lose you the benefit of the doubt when it comes to grading— and you might very well need that benefit.

College teachers are as sensitive as anyone else. Most people like to believe they are good at what they do, and college teachers like to think of themselves as good teachers. Your consistent cutting tells your teacher that you consider him a failure: he isn't sufficiently interesting to get you to come to class. And your teacher—at least on some level—will take it personally. He might take it out on you personally.

Attendance is especially important in seminars, language, math, and science classes. The smaller the class, the more your absences are noticed, so if you have to play hooky, cut a large lecture class. The worst classes to skip are seminars where student participation is expected. Cutting seminars undermines the whole class.

It's also essential to show up regularly to math, science, and language classes. If you are facile with words and know the tricks of extemporaneous writing, you might get by with absences in some of your humanities and social science classes. Math, science, and language classes are different: here, learning is cumulative, with each class building on the previous class. If you fall behind, it becomes increasingly difficult to catch up.

If You Do Cut

Don't make a big deal about it. Professors who require attendance might require a doctor's note or some other justification for your absence. Professors who don't take attendance don't care why you were out.

I never could understand why students bother bringing me notes explaining why they missed a class. I don't read them and I suspect few professors do. (It's another matter if you miss an exam.) Nor do I understand why students bother to tell me they will miss the next class. Why call attention to an absence?

DO THE READINGS

Prepare for class

I know this sounds like more obvious professor talk but believe me, preparation is far from common.

All students are "rah rah" the first week of class. They do the assigned readings and come to class rearing to go. Then the slack-off begins. By the end of the first month a sizable contingent have stopped coming to class prepared. By the end of the second month, you can count on one hand the number of students who read the material before coming to class. By the middle of the third month, forget it; the student who still prepares is now a rarity.

Read the assignments all through the semester and consider yourself an extraordinary phenomenon. College homework is a term-long affair. In high school you did your homework only when it was assigned and when you expected it to get checked. In college, you have to rely on your own schedule and discipline.

Figure it this way: you have to read the material eventually anyway, so you may as well read it before class. It's much more effective that way: even boring classes are improved, and you can contribute to the class.

The big hurdle is reading those stupefying assignments that seem to have been written as prescriptions for sleeping pills. To get these assignments done, you've got to make class preparation part of your daily routine.

But if You Don't Prepare

You won't always come to class prepared. Perhaps you have a test in another class. Or a heavy date the night before. Or a heavy date coming up. What then?

Try not to walk into class totally oblivious of the assignment. Cultivate the art of intelligent skimming; when you get good at it—and like everything else it's a matter of practice—you can pick up lots of information very quickly.

Okay, it was a *very* heavy date. Not only weren't you able to scan the assigned material, you can now barely keep your eyes open. In this situation, it isn't your eyes that matter, it's your mouth. Keep it shut.

Few displays of student behavior are as annoying to teachers as students spouting about subjects they know nothing about—but should, had they done the assigned reading. Don't fool yourself and make a fool of yourself in the process. If you haven't read the article, you don't know it. And if you don't know the assignment, don't advertise that you don't.

WHERE TO SIT

In some large lectures, your seating arrangement is alphabetically determined, so this isn't an issue. But in most classes you have a choice. Where should you sit? Which seat is most conducive to getting the A?

Sit where the action is.

Writers on power often talk about "power centers" in a room. Every class has its corresponding power center. It's the section that carries the weight of the class.

Watch your teacher's movements. (If your teacher is any good, you won't find her sitting behind her desk.) Speakers respond to the section of the audience that responds to them. If one side of the class reacts more vocally to the teacher than the other side, before long, the teacher will be addressing that part of the room more often. Move to that side.

Front or back? You can get an A or an F from the front or the back of the room, but in general, front or toward the front is better.*

Sitting up toward the front has two main advantages:

• **Your professor notices you.** Bad enough that you're a nameless name in the crowd; why be a faceless face in the crowd? Also, teachers tend to think—justifiably or not—that students who sit up front are more conscientious.

• **You insure your participation.** Sitting in the professor's eye-line forces you to behave. Your absences are noticed, so you'll make sure to show up to class. You are also less

---

*Students inform me that some of their professors look out above the first row into the class beyond, so a row or two up might be the best of all.

likely to read, talk, or sleep during even the most boring class. If the class is especially important or particularly dreary, sit up front. You'll need all the help you can get, and this helps.

The worst seat? It's the back corner seat near the door. You seem uninvolved. **If you are stuck in the back, make sure to speak up in class.**

A FEW NOTES ON TAKING NOTES

Unless you have a photographic memory, you need to take some notes. You certainly can't expect to remember during final exam week in May what your professor said back in March.

But don't confuse taking notes with stenography. A good lecture gets you to *reflect* during class. You can't listen, think, and respond if you're busy playing secretary.

Write down key phrases and ideas that will get you to remember what was discussed (in some classes that will mean a lot of writing, in others very little writing).

Many study guides offer instruction on how to take notes effectively. These guides are a waste of time. You take notes to help *you* review when preparing for exams; what helps you might not help others.

A few of the more compulsive of these study guides recommend that students rewrite their notes after each class. They also suggest that you write a summary at the end of each class, restating the essential points of the lecture. Sure, and I recommend that you do a triathlon every morning and read one play by Shakespeare with dinner every evening. Who are we kidding?

The Old Blackboard Reflex

When I feel mischievous in the middle of a lecture, I sometimes turn and write on the board a word such as "in-
eluctable," or the phrase "the cat's meow," or whatever
comes to mind. I look up at the class and, invariably, I see
dozens of students earnestly copying my words into their
notebooks. The assumption: if it's on the blackboard, it's
important.

Agreed, instructors do use the blackboard to highlight important points. But not everything on the board
merits special attention; professors will use the board
gratuitously, as the whim strikes them. Sometimes they
use it just to show the correct spelling of some obscure
word.

Remember, too, that much that isn't on the board appears on the test. Use your judgment, not your reflexes.

Other People's Notes

If you missed class, it's a good idea to borrow someone's
notes, especially in cumulative classes, the kind where
each class builds on the previous one.

**Make sure, though, to borrow the notes immediately
after the missed class.** If you wait until exam time, two
things will happen. First, the notes lose their context, and
you'll have an awful time trying to make sense of them.
Second, getting the notes will be a battle. Your new friends
won't eagerly part with them the night before the final.

Remember, too, not to trust completely in your classmate's notes. She may have gotten it down wrong. She
might have been lost in a sweet fantasy just when the
important stuff was discussed. She might have that photographic memory and not bother with careful notes.

Private Ruminations

In a later chapter, I encourage you to keep a journal of your personal thoughts, a sort of intellectual diary. You should also save a section in the back of your notebook for class-related meditations. Something your professor or a classmate said might trigger an interesting idea. Jot it down. These notes can become extremely helpful when you review for an exam.

LEAVE A MESSAGE AND WE'LL GET BACK TO YOU

When tape recorders first started showing up on my students' desks, I had this terrifying image of lecturing to a classroom empty of people but dotted with little tape recorders on every desk. At the end of this imaginary lecture, my students would come to pick up their tape recorders. After a while, I figured that since no one was responding during class, I might as well just tape my lectures. So I'd bring in my tape recorder, set it up on the lectern, hit "play," and leave; all the other tape recorders would dutifully record my words of wisdom.

An old-fashioned nightmare. Soon, I suppose, video cameras will appear on desks to record lectures. Professors will have to take acting lessons, which, come to think of it, isn't such a bad idea.

Why tape record the class? I suppose that students use tape recorders as a security blanket. They're afraid they might miss something important and feel reassured knowing that the vital information is trapped in that little box, caught forever on a magnetic strip.

Beware: not even narcissistic professors like having

their classes taped. Having your lecture recorded is like having your classes audited by your boss. It kills spontaneity: you're always afraid you might say something incriminating or dumb.

For those who insist on bringing a tape recorder to class, here are a few rules:

- Get your teacher's permission first. It's rude to record anyone without telling him, and rudeness toward the person who grades you isn't clever.
- Don't use a tape recorder if it inhibits you from participating in class. Some students who would otherwise speak up will shut down when they're being recorded.
- Don't rely on the recording. Gestures convey crucial information. Your tape recorder can't capture the body language.

Since you have to listen to the class anyway, why not just pay attention the first time?

CLASS PARTICIPATION

Want to get an A? Participate.

As I've said, showing up to class is essential, and not showing up will hurt your grade. But coming to class isn't enough. According to a recent survey, only 20 percent of the average class asks questions, and you should join this minority if you want to secure the A.

Professors seek, need, and appreciate student involvement in their class. We need applause, and the applause of the classroom is animated discussion. Even the most thick-skinned professor knows when he's not setting his class on fire. Students who make professors feel successful are rewarded with better grades.

Too Shy?

Are you uncomfortable speaking up in a group? What are you going to do about it? Resign yourself to spending four years in silence, masquerading as part of the classroom furniture?

Perhaps you are reluctant to speak up because you don't want to sound like those annoying classmates who blabber inanities in class. You fear that you don't have anything of substance to add to the proceedings.

I know it's difficult, but try not to worry about what your classmates think of you. They won't judge you: they're too busy thinking about their own brilliant comments. Some people are too self-conscious to dance on a crowded floor in a discotheque. There too, no one notices.

A tinge of nervousness before speaking in a group is perfectly normal. Just bear in mind that making a comment in class is no major undertaking—your contribution counts as much as any of your classmate's. And rest assured, it gets easier with practice.

You will need to speak in public when you are out in the world. The college classroom affords a wonderful opportunity to become good at it.

Don't Lecture

About that blabbering classmate: every class has one. He thinks his classmates are paying money to hear him, not the professor, lecture. He has opinions about everything and makes sure everyone knows them. He considers himself provocative—but the only thing he provokes is a conspiracy to lynch.

Typically, this student loves to argue; he argues for the sake of arguing. He's not about the courage of his conviction; he's about contrariness: tell him it's raining and he'll say it's snowing, tell him it's snowing and he'll call it a beach day.

He believes belligerence is endearing, but everyone finds him immature, boring, and self-defeating.

If you genuinely disagree with your professor—and if you aren't catatonic, you'll disagree plenty of times—by all means, voice your objection. But challenging your professor's dominance for the sake of the challenge alone is a no-win strategy. The classroom is the professor's turf, his territorial imperative. **Attempts to undercut his authority bring you only one result: a lower grade.**

Another, milder class nerd is the student who insists on treating the class to private, boring anecdotes about his life. This clod isn't interested in asserting his brilliance; he just considers his personal life endlessly fascinating to everyone. So we have to listen to tales about how his mother tortured him as a child, how his uncle became a Bedouin in the Sahara, how he stopped a mugger on the subway, and how his roommate ripped off the telephone company. Somebody should tell him that **nobody is interested.**

These students don't just irritate their classmates by using the classroom for their personal forum, they deflect the class discussion away from the direction the professor intended. Professors respond by lowering these students' grades.

Questions Are Better Than Comments

Teachers like comments that move the discussion along. They like questions even better, and among the best questions are requests for clarification.

"Could you explain that again?" is not an appropriate question if you didn't understand the discussion because you were busy doing the Sunday crossword puzzle. It is an excellent question if you paid attention and need to have a point repeated. This sort of question does your classmates a service. If you didn't follow what was said, the chances are that many of your classmates didn't either.

Requests for elucidation also help your grade. It shows you care about the material and want to understand the class discussion. But don't overdo it. You don't want to seem obstructive or slow.

Ask Questions about an Upcoming Exam

Has your professor told the class little or no information about the upcoming test? Ask. Wait till the end of class (some professors prefer questions at the end of the class period) and ask your professor what to expect: an essay or short-answer test, or a cumulative, open book exam? Sometimes your instructor doesn't tell the class because she simply forgets to, and your question is a welcome reminder.

Dress

I'd rather not believe that professors factor in a student's appearance in the determination of his or her grade, but studies indicate otherwise. Especially at the grade-school and high-school levels, good-looking students are graded more leniently than ugly students.

I think you are pretty safe dressing as you like in college, and I think you should dress as you like in any case. Don't be surprised, however, if you run into that professor who takes you—and your work—less seriously than you'd like because you wear outlandish clothing.

DEALING WITH BOREDOM

Fact one: You will have to sit through boring classes. Fact two: If you are unlucky, you will sit through many boring classes.

This is the fourth class in which you've discussed the symbolic role of birds in early Anglo-Saxon literature. Moreover, you're a computer science major with less than zero interest in birds, real or symbolic, and you're only taking this class to meet a humanities requirement. You've been good. You've contributed your insights on the relationships between bird chirps and microchips. And you're bored out of your wits.

Don't read. Don't talk. Your professor can see your face, so look alive. Bored or not, the grade counts.

It's time for creativity. Play mind games. Count how many times your teacher uses the work *impact*. Decide who are the three best-looking students in the class. Check out the other students' accents. Picture your professor as a five-year-old . . . as an eighty-year-old.

If you're inventive, you can come up with dozens of mind games that keep you entertained and, at the same time, keep your attention focused on what's happening in class. This has the advantage of making it appear as if you're interested in the class; how could you professor know that when you are looking at him, you're imagining him with a pacifier in his mouth?

THOU SHALT NOT

Here's a review of behavior you must avoid. Etiquette is not the concern here (though that counts too). The concern is how to avoid a lower grade than you deserve.

- **Never badmouth the subject matter.** A quick and sure way to get a lousy grade in a class: ridicule the subject you're studying. You, a twenty-year-old undergraduate, have decided that economics is "bull," or that psychology is all smoke, or that Henry James can't write for beans.

    Your professor has devoted his life to the subject and will judge you to be an ignorant, impudent brat. He will also welcome the opportunity to grade your work as severely as he can.

- **Never study for an exam in another class.** This suggests to the professor that you worry more about the other class than her own. It's insulting.

- **Avoid coming late or leaving early.** In college, you are largely anonymous. To get A's, you need to stand out. But that doesn't include standing out like a sore thumb— arriving late and leaving early are the wrong ways to call attention to yourself.

    Don't stare at your watch, pack your books or put your coat on five minutes before the end of the class. These maneuvers disrupt the class and offend your professor. If you have to leave early, tell your professor before class starts and sit near an exit.

- **Never read in class.** Textbooks from other classes are bad enough, but magazines and newspapers are particularly offensive.

- **Don't sit at your desk without a notebook.** Bring paper and pen even if all you do is doodle. Pretend you are a serious student.

- **Don't yack in class.** It's rude and makes you seem adolescent.

3

Preparing for Exams

Create like a god, command like a king, and work like a slave.

—BRANCUSI

I not only use all the brains that I have, but all that I can borrow.

—WOODROW WILSON

Do old exams help you prepare for tomorrow's test?

What if I despise my textbook?

How can I tell what will be on the test?

You sat down to study at eight o'clock and now it's eleven. Three hours, not bad. But maybe not good enough.

The purpose of studying is to get points on the exam, not with God. The fact that you sat for three hours in front of a book will make you feel virtuous and your parents happy, but it has little to do with getting an A.

Too many books and advisors make a big deal about setting aside a few hours a day for study and the importance of rigorously sticking to your schedule. The objective becomes the amount of time spent sitting in a chair and not what you accomplished while you sat there. That is all wrong. Your professor doesn't know how long you studied and he doesn't care. What he cares about (and what you are tested on) is your understanding of the course work. Studying is piecework, not timework.

Your objective should not be "I will sit and study for an hour and a half," but "I need to learn how to find the slope of a line." Your assignment might take you six hours or six minutes, and what takes you six minutes might take someone else six hours.

Examinations test your knowledge, not your effort; count the pages, not the hours.

DISCIPLINE

Once you've carved out a reasonable chunk of material to study, you've got to sit down and do the work.

Studying is a drag. Who wants to read something because someone is going to test you on it? Studying, like washing dishes, mowing lawns, and filling out forms, is something you do only because you have to.

If you share this bad attitude toward studying, almost anything will distract you. Do I hear a leaf rustle? Did someone open an eyelid? Harder still is fighting off the more compelling temptations to raid the refrigerator for a snack, call Fred on the phone, and flip over the record to side two.

I can't tell you how to channel the willpower you will need to study . . . when you figure that out let me know. What I can tell you is that, one way or another, you will need that willpower. If you ever managed to get into a jogging routine or stick to a diet, you have what it takes to study regularly. Do you remember the little speech you gave yourself when you adopted those other positive habits? Well, give yourself that speech once again.

If you still have trouble getting yourself to study, take a stroll over to your local bookstore and head for the pop psychology section. That's the shelf with the books telling you how wonderful you are and how you shouldn't let yourself get pushed around by all those miserable creatures who make up the rest of humanity. That section also features two dozen books explaining the newest in behavior modification techniques, guaranteed to teach you self-control.

Have fun browsing, but don't buy any of them—I'll save you a couple of bucks. The wisdom of those two dozen books boils down to two useful recommendations in your attempt to slay the "study dragon."

- Don't bite off more than you can chew. You are not going to read the whole textbook tonight. Delineate a reasonable amount of work, read it, and then, satisfied with yourself, go hang out with the new love of your life.
- Reward yourself for good work. Take the money you almost spent on the pop psychology book and buy yourself a treat. But remember—and this is the second point—reward yourself *after*, not before, you do your work.

Work Hard and Play Hard but Not at the Same Time

When you work, *work*; when you play, *play*. If you let the play seep into your study, you won't get much work done and then, when you go out to play, you'll feel guilty all night for not having studied enough. The net total is little study and little fun.

College students are remarkably adept at fooling themselves about studying. If you can concentrate on cell biology while listening to music with lyrics, you either have lousy taste in music or you're not studying very hard. Perhaps you can walk and chew gum at the same time, but you cannot study accounting while having that heart-to-heart telephone conversation with Kim.

Determine *when* you get your best work done. Seven in the morning? Ten at night? Biorhythms differ, so don't let others' routines persuade you to do the same. Determine, too, *where* you work most efficiently. Most Homo sapiens study best in a private carrel in the library or in the woods away from the maddening crowds. If *you* do your best studying in a shower stall, in Grand Central Station, or hanging from a chandelier, then by all means move to where the work gets done.

Study for the Hard Courses and the Heavy Credits

We are a weak-willed species. Why do the hard when you can do the easy? Why study for the statistics test when you can study for that fun class in cinema studies?

The answer is straightforward: If you don't study for the statistics test, you will fail the course. Grit your teeth, do your hard subjects first, and do them thoroughly.

Make sure, too, that you apportion your studying to the number of credits of each class. Your A in a one-credit course won't offset a D in a four-credit class; indeed, you have a higher index if you receive a D in your one-credit class and a lowly C in your four-credit class. Study not what you want, but what you must. In the best possible world, these are the same subjects; in our less than perfect world, you take classes out of necessity, not love. Those credits count just as much, though.

MATERIALS

The Textbook

Most textbooks are boring. Textbooks are supposed to present "just the facts" without editorial opinion (at least without blatant opinion), but "just the facts" often has the effect of a handful of sedatives. A chronology of the geological ages isn't the sort of reading that keeps college students glued to their desks.

Here are five things to do while studying from your textbook. They won't transform your textbook into a thriller, but they will help make your study session more productive.

- Approach the book systematically. First get an overview of the chapter length and the author's writing style to see what you are up against. Then skim the chapter headings and subheadings and the sidebars (that's the writing in the margins). After you've gotten the lay of the land, go back to the beginning and start reading; this way you know where you're headed.
- I find it useful to write notes when I study, but others prefer underlining. Perhaps the best part of this exercise is that it keeps your mind from straying into distant daydreams.
- At the end of each study session, write a list of definitions and key phrases. This list turns into a considerable bonus when you review for the test.

- Charts and graphs deserve more than a cursory glance. They offer a concise visual summary of the text and will jar your memory during exams. (If you aren't good at reading graphs, get good at it. You will need this skill throughout college.)
- Pay particular attention to the textbook if your professor "teaches the text." His exams will most likely come straight from the textbook as well.

Use a Different Textbook

"Professors use three textbooks: one to assign to their class, another from which to steal lectures, and a third from which to steal test questions."

Your professor assigned the class textbook primarily because he is familiar with it and has probably used the same text for half a century. Another possibility is that his friend wrote the book, and your professor feels obliged to do his friend a favor. Whatever the reason, and whatever the merits of the book, don't limit yourself to it.

Study from another textbook in addition to the one used in your class. You might luck out and get just that one from which your professor "steals his exams," but even if not, the advantages of studying from another textbook are plentiful.

An additional textbook is helpful not only for reading, but also as a source of exercises and quizzes. These problems and their solutions provide a wonderful way of testing yourself to see if you are prepared for the exam. (In the sciences especially, make sure to choose a textbook that isn't outdated.)

Another nice thing about supplemental textbooks is that they are free. Your college library will always have several textbooks sitting unloved and untouched in the stacks.

Another source is a friend who took the same course with a different professor and used a different textbook.

Read Secondary Sources

Secondary material is articles and books written about the articles and books you are studying. *Many of your professors will explicitly discourage you from looking up secondary material when studying. Do it anyway.*

Most professors, including the ones who tell *you* not to, use secondary material in preparing their lectures. They realize how helpful this resource is and you will too.

Suppose you have to read Kant for an upcoming philosophy exam but find the material so incomprehensible that you have to turn to the title page to make sure you've been reading an English version of the book (Kant isn't much easier to read in the original German). The solution is to find and read a book on the history of philosophy with a section on Kant or a textbook that discusses Kant. After you have absorbed this easier presentation, you can tackle your primary reading assignment.

Here's another example of how it's done. You've got an exam coming up on *Crime and Punishment*. You've read the novel and think you understand it just fine. (Always try to read the primary material before secondary sources.) Go to the library and head for the literature section. Look for the books on Dostoyevski and select a few that have a chapter devoted to *Crime and Punishment*. Your familiarity with the story will make reading this secondary material a pleasure; in turn, reading the secondary material will make your performance on tomorrow's exam a knockout. You will sound erudite, informed, and you'll impress the corduroy patches off your professor's jacket sleeves.

Secondary sources serve two useful functions. They confirm that you've grasped the basic idea—or let you know that you haven't. They also provide new insights. After all, authors of critical texts have spent years of their life analyzing the text, while you've only spent an hour and a half. You might as well make use of their lifetime work.

If possible, read reviews of the book you are studying. Many of the books you are asked to read were reviewed in magazines. Magazine reviews are easy and breezy. (To help you locate their whereabouts use the *Reader's Guide to Periodical Literature.*)

As you might already have realized in the case of movie reviews, reviews are much more fun *after* you've read the book. Having seen the flick, you can read the review and knowledgeably decide whether the critic is brilliantly insightful or a dumb jackass. You can do the same thing with books.

Incidentally, don't limit these magazine visits to works of fiction. A great way to help you study for a course in modern history is to read issues of *Time, Newsweek,* and other magazines of the period you're studying. News writing has a different tinge than history writing; it's "history on the run." You will enjoy seeing pictures of your favorite historical characters, and have even more fun discovering, from the vantage point of the future, how journalists are consistently so wrong in their predictions.

STUDY GROUPS

A committee called the Harvard Assessment Seminar produced a study in 1990 with the catchy title, "Explorations with Students and Faculty about Teaching, Learning, and Student Life." The study uncovered and confirmed a few interesting notions about study groups and other student likes and dislikes.

Students, it seems, do better when they are offered "frequent checkpoints," such as quizzes, homework assignments, and oral exams. Since this would require professors to mark papers all term long, the likelihood of this becoming standard procedure is about the same as the pope judging this year's Miss America pageant. Most professors are far too lazy ("busy" is the way they would put it) for any commitment this laborious.

The Harvard study also recommended study groups. According to the seminar's researchers, students who join study groups find these associations very helpful and get better grades.

Many study groups are disguised social get-togethers, sort of a ladies auxiliary meeting for college students. They start out with an intention to study but quickly disintegrate into bull sessions. In math, science, and economics you can tell when the group has moved from work to prattle; what does Mel Gibson's love life have to do with photosynthesis? When the course is the Victorian novel, it's easier to rationalize the gossip.

It's fine to join a study group to improve your social life, but you still have to get your studying done. Make sure that the *study* facet is as strong as the *group* facet of your study group.

If you join a study group, become a leader not a follower. Teaching is far and away the best way to learn. If you want to have that theorem down pat, try explaining it to someone else. Do you really understand what your professor was talking about in his discussion of "deconstruction"? Express the concept in your own words. Don't think, "I do understand the basic idea; I just have a hard time putting it into words." You'll be fooling yourself. The old maxim is true: If you can't explain it to someone else, you don't understand it yourself.

THE WEEKS AHEAD/
THE NIGHT BEFORE

Keep a Calendar of Upcoming Exams

Some people are list crazy. They even keep lists of lists. The last time I tried to keep a list of things to do, I promptly lost the list. As far as I can tell, organized people don't need lists, and disorganized people, such as myself, never use them.

Nonetheless, I do recommend that you note your upcoming exams on your calendar. This way the "night before" doesn't suddenly spring up on you.

You have many exams during the course of the term and it's common for students to forget when they have which exams. A calendar with the dates of upcoming tests inscribed will frighten you into an early study schedule. Next Tuesday—the management midterm, Thursday—the abnormal psych test . . . you can see their fangs and they're getting closer and closer.

Cramming

"There are two ways of studying for exams: cramming or by not studying at all."

I assume you are a normal college student and, therefore, I assume you will cram before exams. You will cram even though you promised yourself after the last time that you would study all term long and avoid another all-nighter. Now it's finals week, and once again you're ready with six gallons of coffee to get you through the night.

Those who warn against cramming argue that cramming is only good for short-term memory and that you forget most of what you learn soon after the exam. So what? Your concern now is tomorrow morning, not next week. Anyway, before long you forget most of what you learned in college no matter how slowly you learned it.

You *will* cram. The immediate question is, should you stay up all night to do it? Expert opinions differ. Some researchers claim that you need sleep to think clearly, while others insist that a lack of one night's sleep has no appreciable effect on your IQ. Some advise that you refresh yourself with a few hours of sleep, while others argue that a break for an hour or two of sleep will make you even more tired.

You own biological clock should decide. I had a hard time concentrating on math problems after a night of no sleep but otherwise was able to handle a sleepless night without too much difficulty (this is no longer true). How about you? You'll have to find out for yourself.

It is unwise to rely on cramming for learning new material. Cramming is fine as a review, for memorization, but not as your first introduction to a subject. Effective learning needs time to marinate. Cramming is an especially bad crutch when studying for a test in a mathematics or language course. These subjects require incremental learning; one thing builds on another, and if you don't understand the more basic concept, you can't move on to the next level. In these classes, make sure to give yourself ample time to learn the subject thoroughly.

A final point about cramming: Don't mix alcohol or marijuana with cramming. Alcohol on deprived sleep significantly reduces acuity. The standard formula is one drink equals an hour of sleep lost, but for many, the combination of alcohol and sleep deprivation is even more devastating. Marijuana makes the trivial seem profound. Perhaps every trivial insight is profound in some larger context (is this a trivial or profound point?) but you can't afford to lose hours of your precious time ruminating on a passing trifle when you have a major exam at ten tomorrow morning.

Celebrate after the exam, not before.

Old Exams

Should you try to get a copy of your professor's earlier tests? Of course you should.

Old exams are the very best guide to tomorrow's exam. Studying from last year's tests is both "educationally" proper and morally proper. If your instructor is too lazy to invent a new test, that's his problem and to your benefit.

In fact, you should study old exams even if tomorrow's exam is new. The content might change some, but the expectations won't. How much does this professor expect his students to know? What is the expected ratio of memory to analysis?

Old exams are a major find. Share them with a friend.

WHAT WILL BE ON THE TEST

What kind of test should you prepare for? A detailed, fine-combed exam, or a wide-open essay test? What do you think your professor looks for: scintillating originality or an echo of her lectures?

Some professors share detailed information about an upcoming test while others are poker-faced. In the latter case, you need to rely on psychological insight into your professor. If you've attended class regularly, you should have a pretty good idea of your teacher's personality, her likes and dislikes, and the way she reasons.

How do professors decide what kind of exam to give? Let me give you an example—myself.

I give tests for three reasons. First, it is the most effective way to determine a student's grade; second, it is the best way to get students to study; and third, it tells me whether I've taught successfully. But I don't enjoy giving tests, and except for the sadistic few who eventually outgrow it, neither do other professors.

My first decision is whether to give a short-answer test or an essay test. Short-answer tests are harder to create but a breeze to mark, while essay tests are easy to devise but a chore to mark. The aspect of grading I dislike most is grading, so the kind of test I devise depends, in part, on how badly I want to avoid grading that week.

The course material also contributes to the structure of the exam. In philosophy exams—the courses I teach—I measure my students' ability to analyze problems and argue cogently. Multiple choice questions won't pry out that student profile. But straight essays are an invitation to straight bulling, so I usually end up with a mixed bag: a few "describe, explain briefly" questions, a few multiple choice questions, and an essay or two. (After all these years, my exams are still far too long.)

That's my story and my classes know it well before exams. Other professors have their own agendas. Pay attention to your professor's teaching style and personality and you can make a shrewd guess about the kind of test he favors.

ANXIOUS? THAT'S GOOD

Mild anxiety produces what psychologists call "heightened perception." Anxiety gets your adrenalin flowing, which makes you more focused, and focus is good for learning. So if you're worried about tomorrow's exam, at least don't worry that you're worried.

At the Test

Get the facts first. You can distort them later.
—MARK TWAIN

Here are fifteen reminders and suggestions to bring with you to the exam room. It also helps to bring some knowledge of the course material.

1. ARRIVE EARLY

It takes time to settle down before a test, and you'd rather do that before the exam period begins than after. An early arrival also ensures that you're at the right place at the right time.

Another reason for getting to the room a few minutes before the gavel drops is to participate in the flurry of information that sometimes develops right before an exam. A classmate mentions interesting tidbits about an earlier exam given by your professor, or another classmate explains how to solve a problem that had you stymied for days. The professor might grace the room with an early appearance, answer last-minute questions, and offer broad hints about the upcoming exam.

Don't come too early if sitting in an exam room makes you anxious, but make sure not to come late. In addition to the obvious disadvantages of losing time and having to settle for the only remaining seat—the tipsy one with two legs in the hallway—you might also miss crucial information about the exam. Begrudgingly, your proctor will repeat the instructions he gave the class when the exam began, but he'll give them to you in a hurried whisper. You might miss something important.

2. SIT WHERE YOU CAN CONCENTRATE

We're asking for an hour or so of concentration. Don't set yourself up for distractions. The activity on the great lawn probably is more interesting than your business law exam, so don't sit near the window. And while you're deciding where to sit, why not select a seat away from your talking buddies and also beyond staring range of the gorgeous classmate you've eyed all term long. This is an exam; you can manage undivided attention to it for an hour, no?

3. WRITE WITH BLACK OR BLUE INK

It's trivial and obvious, and I wouldn't bother to mention it if I didn't have a few students in every class who submit tests written in pencil or bright-colored ink. A trifle or not, this is the reality: write in iridescent pink and you can forget the A. And don't doodle flowers and little faces in the margins, either.

4. LOOK OVER THE WHOLE TEST BEFORE YOU BEGIN TO WRITE

Begin with a careful reading of the instructions. Instructions not only tell you what you have to do but often give clues on how to do it.

Then quickly read through the exam. A question in the second part of the exam might illuminate a question in the first part and vice versa. This is rather common: questions contain names, ideas, quotes, and data that are useful throughout the test.

5. ALLOCATE YOUR TIME INTELLIGENTLY

Exam questions aren't all worth equal points and don't deserve equal time. Invariably, I will get a few test booklets with three pages of writing for a ten-point question that called for "a brief explanation" and only one page for the twenty-five-point essay question. Students surmise that if the ten-pointer is the only essay they can answer well, they'll give that question all they've got and just zip through the other questions.

That's a foolish calculation. The dazzling analysis on the lower point problem won't brighten your dismal work on the higher point problem. You are better off with a few points less on each question than full credit on the lower point question and none for the question worth much more.

Wear a watch; at the outset of the test you can determine

how you will allocate your time. If part I is worth thirty points, it should take about 30 percent of your time.

6. USE ALL THE EQUIPMENT YOU'RE PERMITTED TO USE

If you are one of those people who thinks only wimps use novocaine before getting a tooth cavity filled, this isn't for you. This suggestion is directed to the rest of the species, who believe pain is not something to cheer about and who accept needed help when it's offered.

If you are allowed to use your calculator, use it. If you are permitted to use your books or notes, use them too. (Careful: Don't deplete your time by turning the opportunity into a study session.) You are competing with students who are availing themselves of this help, and you aren't going to get extra points for *not* using these tools.

Another precious tool you can use is a piece of paper designated for scrap. Use it to pin down those meteoric ideas that flash through your mind during exams. Jot down those important names and phrases, and you won't spend the rest of the exam fretting that you won't remember the information when you need it.

7. DO THE EASY QUESTIONS FIRST

We'll repeat this when we get to the different types of tests, but here's the general rule: answer first what you know best. This way you get working quickly, you build up confidence, and you'll have the extra time to spend on the tougher questions.

8. ANSWER EVERY QUESTION

On some standardized tests, you get points off for wrong answers. That's rarely the case in college—it makes tallying up your grade too complicated for most professors.

In multiple choice or true/false tests, where a correct random choice counts as much as a knowledgeable choice, it's stupid to leave a question unanswered—you gain nothing by leaving the answer blank. But even when you are faced with an essay question that has you bewildered, a creative response might gain you some points. In math and science tests, your problem-solving work will also help your grade.

9. LEAVE SPACE FOR COMMENTS

Why do some students submit test booklets with their scrawl extending beyond the margins north and west, covering every millimeter of space? Are they trying to make sure that the professor has no place to write his comments?

It's a bad idea, in any case. First, by depriving yourself of your grader's comments you won't learn from your mistakes. Second, it's frustrating for the grader to have no room for comments about your work, and a frustrated grader is not in your interest. Swim in the prescribed lanes.

10. ASK CREATIVE/DEVIOUS QUESTIONS

This is one of the few suggestions I'm reluctant to include in this book, not because it will make things better for you, but because it will make things worse for me. Professors don't relish the parade of students waiting to ask them "just one quick question, please," in the midst of an exam.

On occasion, a student will find a genuine flaw in the test, and the teacher will need to make a clarification to the whole class. Usually, though, the questions are rhetorical and a waste of time. The questions demonstrate either that the student hasn't read, heard, or understood the instructions or simply doesn't know the answer.

The sort of question I *am* suggesting you might ask is one that will help you without playing up your ignorance. You quietly ask, "Is it okay if I answer number three by discussing how . . . ?" Or, "In choice 'b' in question six, I'm assuming that you mean so-and-so and not so-and-so." These questions are just undercover requests for details; I'm asked either to supply some needed information or to confirm what the student thinks is true.

This method of ferreting information is known as the complex question. It is a venerable weapon in the lawyer's arsenal. He asks the witness, "Have you stopped beating your wife?" or "Would you tell the court where you hid the money you stole? Please answer yes or no." The question smuggles in an admission of guilt and the poor guy is damned whether he answers yes or no.

If you disguise your question poorly, your professor will see it for what it is—a request for the answer—and he will just turn away. But if you formulate a sharp question that sounds legitimate (this takes subtlety), you will walk back to your seat with a pretty good idea of the correct answer.

Come to the test prepared and you won't have to resort to this sort of scheme. If you do resort to it, don't try it more than once per exam.

11. CHECK FOR CARELESS
MISTAKES CAREFULLY

Do careless mistakes count? Should they?

Students argue that it is unfair to take points off for a micro-oversight. This was a calculus exam, designed to test one's ability to find a derivative, not the ability to multiply seven by four. The same argument applies to a humanities or social science exam: This was a test devoted to the Russian Revolution, not English orthography—why lose points for a misspelling?

Students accept the importance of details. "Agreed," says the student spokesperson, "I'll remind my mother to teach me the virtue of caring for the small matters as well as the large. But this professor's job is to teach math or history, not the virtues. It's certainly not what the test is about."

The professor sees it differently. "Paying attention to the details is crucial to mathematics [botany, music, anthropology, et cetera] and it's part of my job to teach the importance of this attitude by penalizing even minor oversights."

Both viewpoints are plausible. But in this pedagogical debate, being right doesn't matter. This is one of those situations where might, not right, makes the decision, and your professor is the one with the might. Many professors take points off, explicitly or implicitly, for careless lapses. Review your work before submitting it.

12. STAY THE DURATION

Those students who leave the exam room early usually do poorly on their tests. If the test is all short answers, you need to review your answers for careless errors. If the exam contains essay questions, or science or math problems, you need to make sure you've covered the bases and didn't neglect any essential steps.

You don't have to stay until the bitter end, but don't feel pressured to rush out even if many of your classmates are packing it in early. Take your time.

13. WRITE YOUR NAME ON EACH BOOKLET YOU SUBMIT

Most students are pretty good about writing their names on their first test booklet, but a few forget to write their name on their second booklet. The frantic search begins. The second booklet was somehow misplaced and now the professor has to find out where and to whom it belongs.

It's not your fault, but the annoyance will be charged against you anyway. Prevent the inconvenience by writing your name on each booklet you submit.

14. SAVE YOUR TEST QUESTIONS

Most professors let you keep the test questions, and you should do so for at least a year. (Many professors are reluctant to let you keep multiple choice questions because they want to avoid the gruelling work of devising a new set every semester.)

If you ever take the same professor in the future, you can remind yourself of this professor's test style. You certainly should keep the midterm exam as an important document in preparing for the final exam.

15. THIS IS ONLY A TEST

Did you ever try to remember someone's name to absolutely no avail and then have it emerge, unannounced, later on? Trying to remember a name is the worst way to recall it: you expend a lot of "mental energy" that detracts from remembering. (It's like trying to fall asleep; you have to stay up to make the effort.)

Mild anxiety is helpful for learning but not helpful for recalling information on a test. It's important that you take your exam in a state of relative calm rather than agitation. Use whatever relaxation technique works for you, but don't overdo it. You want to be loose, not asleep.

5

The Essay Exam

Garbage is garbage, but the history of garbage is scholarship.

What's the best way to prepare for the essay exam?

What is the best and worst way to begin an essay? To conclude an essay?

How do I write an essay when I don't know what I'm talking about?

They are in my class every term. Bright, articulate students who ask the right questions and clearly know their stuff, yet manage only a mediocre B or less on their exams. Why? Because they can't write a decent essay.

If you can't write a quality essay, you can't ace college. Conversely, if you *can* write a quality essay, not only will you excel in the classes for which you are prepared, you will also get by in those classes for which you are not prepared.

SUBJECTIVE ELEMENTS

The grading of essays is, in large measure, subjective. The grader has some general notion of what he expects you to discuss, but beyond that he relies on his "feeling" of whether or not you have answered appropriately. The high A and the low F are objective, but everything in between depends on personal judgment.

Luck, too, plays a role in your essay's grade. For example, your fine essay will seem just average if the essay right before it was brilliant; that one got an A, making it harder to give you the same grade for your lesser work. But if your routine essay follows a dim-witted essay, your work, in contrast, will seem superior.

Neither can you plan for your professor's mood, expansive and generous or picky and strict. If your teacher's kid just turned the kitchen wall into an abstract expressionist mural, don't be surprised if he takes it out on your essay. But it's your lucky day if, just as your professor turns to grade your essay, she finds out that her cherished article has been accepted for publication.

You can't control luck, but you can control the other, more important, subjective factors that decide your grade. To achieve this control you need to understand the strategy that underlies winning essays.

The Grader's Perspective

The key to writing the A essay is to put yourself in your professor's seat. Your task is not to write the outstanding essay but to write the essay that impresses the professor as outstanding.

Write an essay that jumps out of that pile, that stands out from the crowd. *While your essay is the only one you submit, it's just one of thirty-four that your professor grades*. Burying your essay in the pack by writing a quiet, commonplace essay invites a medium grade.

Remember, too, grading is drudgery. When your professor confronts those thirty-four essays he has but one desire: to get it over with. The less painful to read, the greater the appreciation.

With that in mind, let's turn our attention to preparing for the essay exam.

WRITE OUT THE ESSAY THE NIGHT BEFORE

What essay? After all, unless your professor is exceptionally easy—or you a very adroit thief—you won't know the essay question before the exam.

Write a generic essay. Think up a solid, general question that covers the material you need to study and write out the answer. Not just key words, not just an outline, write *a full-fledged, full-bodied essay*. It is very important that you do this, so try to understand why.

Writing gets you to think clearly.

You've been told all your life to "think before you speak," but it isn't helpful advice. In fact, it's not even meaningful advice: we think *by* speaking. True, on formal occasions we formulate our exact words before saying them, but even then we speak the words beforehand, if only to ourselves. In most of our life, we just talk and somehow the words are there. If you doubt this, try to compose your sentences before you express them during your next conversation. You will find yourself saying little, if anything at all. (Not a bad idea in some cases.)

To think clearly, think out loud. Ideas are cloudy, shapeless blobs until given form in speech or writing. If you can't say it, you can't whistle it either. So if you are working out some complex idea, go for a walk and "talk-out" your thoughts; this will help crystallize your thinking, give it structure and precision.

Nothing beats writing for achieving clarity. In the initial stages of studying, it's okay to just let ideas emerge free-form, but when you need to get past this early, murky phase, write your thoughts down. In the process of writing, you overcome waffling and commit yourself to a point of view.

Writing the details is crucial to this exercise. It's not enough to note that Freud thought dreams were important, with the expectation that you can fill in the sordid details during the exam tomorrow. Unless you spell them out now, you can't be sure that you really have them under your belt; tomorrow will be too late.

If you get lucky, the essay question will resemble the one you wrote last night. Bull's-eye! More likely, you won't have the opportunity to reproduce your evening's essay in its entirety, but with clever bending, shaping, and well-placed connections, you can graft whole chunks of your prepared essay onto your exam.

Writing out essays beforehand is the best way to study for an essay exam.

FIRST MOVES

The class quiets down, and you have your test paper in hand. You quickly skim the instructions, take pen to hand, read the first essay and start writing.

You've got it all wrong. Not only will your headlong rush to write cost you time in the long run, it will also cost you points. You have a number of important decisions to make before you begin writing.

Instructions

Read the instructions. Carefully.

At least once a year, a student will answer three essays when I asked for only two. Because this student didn't have the patience to read through the instructions, he squandered precious time.

Instructions suggest what kind of essay is expected: how specific, whether you need to refer to the readings, whether to include your own opinion. A smart reading of the instructions detects helpful clues.

Read All the Essay Questions

Examine all the questions before you answer any of them. This has several benefits.

You manage your time wisely.

Students sometimes believe that as long as they fill up the test booklet, it won't matter that they only answered one question completely. The ploy doesn't work—answer *each* essay as required, Remember, too, that not all essay questions are worth equal points, and not all require equal time.

You find hidden information.

Essay three might have information, explicit or buried, that you need for essay one and vice versa. Some phrase in one essay question triggers the memory of something else you need for another essay; these associations are hard to predict but they show up regularly.

Make notes on scrap paper as you read the questions. Jot down ideas as they pop into your head and this way

you won't worry about forgetting them later when you
need them. You might prefer to dedicate the last page of
your booklet for random scribblings: include here all your
associations, allusions, definitions, and comments, both
used and discarded. Remember to cross out your work
before handing in the test booklet.

You can begin with your best essay.

You scout the exam and survey the task ahead. Essay two
is your baby, you know this stuff inside out, perfecto.
Essay one you have a handle on, but it's going to take
some heavy-duty creativity to pull it together. Essay three
looks like ancient Turkish. Which essay do you begin with?

Do your best essay first. First impressions are invalu-
able, so lead with the essay you know best. Your weaker
essays will be graded more leniently if they are seen as
coming from a student who knows his stuff. Beginning with
what you know also has the psychological advantage of
building the confidence you'll need when you hit the mud-
dier waters.

If it's a close call between two essays, and one of those
essays is the first choice on the question sheet, I'd go with
that one. When you skip the first essay and do it later,
you imply that you aren't fully on top of the question. I
wouldn't worry about this too much—often the professor
himself doesn't remember the order of questions.

Write an Essay Outline

You are still not ready to write your essay. Reading the
instructions and the essay questions has cost you but a
minute or two, and you will need to spend a couple of
minutes more writing an outline before you begin to write
your essay.

I expect you to balk at this suggestion. You think that writing an outline is an unnecessary waste of time and time is one thing you can't fritter away during an exam. I agree that time is one thing you can't afford to waste, which is why you should write an outline. Writing an outline *saves* you time!

Without a written outline, you assemble a few random thoughts, write any old innocuous first sentence, manage a paragraph or two, and then come to a grinding halt. Where to go next? Ideas come to mind in a disjointed, meandering fashion, and when you write them as they come to mind, the result is an essay that's disjointed and meandering. Without an outline, you swim in circles, ending up exhausted and nowhere.

We aren't talking here about a decked out outline complete with Roman numerals and indented letters but only about a sketch of the main ideas you want to discuss and the order in which you want to discuss them. You aren't submitting the outline (you still need to write a full-blown, full-sentenced essay) so write it fast and ugly and deviate from this outline when so inclined. An outline prepares you for writing a substantial opening sentence. As we will see soon, this first sentence is extremely important in the determination of your grade. In addition, if you run out of time, you can incorporate the outline into your essay. Again, more about this later.

STRUCTURING THE IMPRESSIVE ESSAY

Let me remind you again, because this is central to writing the winning essay: professors don't like grading essay exams. It's not surprising—who wants to read a hundred undergraduate essays a year, year after year?

The trick, then, is to quickly demonstrate your command of the question. How do you do that?

Indicate a Mastery of Scope

Set up categories and divide your essay into sections. This suggests that you have the big picture in focus. Let me give you an example. Suppose on a history test you're asked the (far too broad) question: "What were the causes of the Korean War?" Begin your answer by saying that you will approach the issue from three perspectives: political, social, and economic. Most impressive, indeed. You are a student who sees the broader picture, and can deal with the subject systematically. You've already made at least a B!

With creativity, you can construct appropriate categories for every subject in which you write an essay.

Discuss Opposing Views Seriously

College professors adore student essays that vigorously present the opposing point of view. Why? Because interesting problems invite debate and rarely have definitive solutions. Your essay will gleam when you give the opposition a fair shake.

Such fair-mindedness is uncommon in college essays. Students who do argue the other side usually set up straw men to kick around. The opposition is constructed of such weak arguments that they are crushed with the drop of a feather. Give both sides the strongest defense you can muster, and you'll show intellectual maturity. You will also ace the essay.

Give the Essay Your Personal Spin— Moderately

Should you write your own ideas or just spit back your professor's ideas? This is a very delicate decision.

Tests that demand only the professor's own opinions are memory quizzes, not real tests of knowledge. Many professor delight in their own words and anticipate seeing them on your exam paper. If that's what they want, that's what they should get.

You can make an educated guess whether your professor is one of these megalomaniacs. Does he invite comment in class and treat opposing opinions with respect? Does he encourage open-minded student thinking? These are the best indications of what he looks for on a test.

Take note: Even professors who welcome your opinion in class don't want to see much of it on exams.

Your teacher doesn't care about your opinion. Yes, of course, he values your right to an opinion. He respects that fact that you have an opinion. He might even value your opinion about other subjects, but he doesn't value your opinion in *his* area of expertise, the subject of the test. And why should he? It is absurd to expect that you, a student in an undergraduate course, are going to answer a problem he and his colleagues have been working on for fifteen years. You can impress him with your perceptiveness and understanding, but do not expect to become a professional with your first essay or term paper. It's adolescent arrogance. You don't walk on the tennis court for the first time in your life and triumph at Wimbledon. I tell you this not to undermine your self-assurance but to secure that A.

What follows? **Present your view only after you have made it clear that you have done the readings and mas-**

tered the material. I get back too many essays with three hurried sentences addressing the essay question, and fifty sentences of personal opinion. Your opinion is secondary—treat it that way.

When you do offer your own analysis, show humility. Write your essay seriously, but don't think it deserves serious attention. Your professor is reading your essay only because it's on a test. What's in question is your understanding of the material and your ability to compose a reasoned personal viewpoint. Meet these requirements and that is all.

THE CRUCIAL FIRST SENTENCE: A FIRST AND LASTING IMPRESSION

Your opening sentence is the most important sentence in your essay. Professors often skim the rest of the essay, but they read your first sentence.

Demonstrate at the outset that you are in command of the essay, and your later errors may be missed or discounted. An inferior beginning, on the other hand, means lower expectations, and you will need an outstanding essay to overcome this psychological barrier.

Begin authoritatively with substance. Avoid the mealy-mouthed, meaningless pronouncement. "This is a problem that has plagued mankind for centuries" is the kind of empty phrase students use to kick-start their engines. It isn't false, but the unimpressive implication is that you are feeling your way into the essay.

Repeating the question is another favored stalling technique. The question calls for a discussion of the economic effects of the corruption in the Harding administration, and you begin your essay with, "The corruption in the Harding administration had important effects on the economy." No kidding. (People stall this way in conversation too. You ask them a question and they repeat it to give themselves time to come up with an answer. It's annoying in oral discourse, but worse in written discourse.)

When you waver in the opening, you wave the reader on until she gets to the meat of your essay. By then, your essay has lost points. Your opening sentence should always make a favorable impression.

THE LAST SENTENCE: THE CONCLUDING IMPRESSION

Let's jump from the beginning to the conclusion, the second most important sentence in your essay. These are the last words of your essay that the professor reads before deciding your grade. Make them count.

Last sentences are read, even by professors who only read the opening sentences and flit around the rest of the essay. In addition to the legitimate endings, professors often find intriguing messages attached to the conclusion. These additions are usually pitiful pleas. A typical supplication: "Please be easy on me when you grade this. The day you discussed this topic in class, I was out with an acute case of acutites." Sometimes the appeal is more poignant: "Please be easy on my grade. I shouldn't be here today. I have a high fever due to my acute acutites."

As with the opening sentence, don't spin the wheels at the end of your essay either. Avoid such barren proclamations as, "This problem will continue to plague mankind for many years ahead." (What an awesome essay. It begins with the insight that the problem has been around for centuries and ends by telling us that it will continue for centuries to come, which makes you wonder what the point was of all those words in the middle of the essay.)

A vacuous ending is inadvisable, but so is the one that brings up something entirely new. The introduction of a whole new idea at this point undercuts what preceded it and makes your essay seem disorganized. Instead, end your essay with an interesting suggestion that follows from the points you have raised in your core answer to the essay question.

WHAT *NOT* TO DO IN AN ESSAY

Avoid Vagueness

You want to show your professor that you are in control of the essay, but you weaken that impression when you use words that indicate hesitancy. Here are two examples of vague words to avoid:

Basically. This is, basically, one of the worst words you can use in an essay. "Basically, what Skinner is saying . . . " sounds as if you aren't sure what Skinner is saying. Fudging doesn't get an A.

Sort of/kind of. These words, too, suggest a lack of confidence. "Aristophanes is sort of poking fun at the Homeric gods" doesn't tell us whether you think he is or isn't. Hedging doesn't get an A either.

A lack of conviction will show up anyway—there's no need to advertise it.

Avoid Street Jargon

Professors like their own jargon, not yours.

Each professor has his own hate list of plebeian, lazy

words which he will pounce on when they show up in your essay. For example, at the top of my hate list is the word "into," as in "Mailer is into the writing of Hemingway." Into? Do you mean interested in, committed to, concerned with, absorbed by, engrossed, preoccupied, intrigued, immersed, involved? Other words on my loathe list are "finalize" or "impact" used as a verb.

Your exam essay isn't the occasion to rehearse your hip, street-talk writing style; save it for the school literary magazine. Write in the standard, classical mode.

Avoid Sesquipedalian Words

Don't move to the other end of the jargon scale either.

The touch of righteous meanness residing in the bosoms of all mankind lurks in your professors' fibres as well. This professorial meanness erupts when they read student essays strewn with bigshot words, used in place of simpler and more direct words. Write simply and to the point. When you use "high falutin" language, your professor starts paying attention to *how* you say what you say, not *what* you say.

This point is more serious that it appears. When you show off, you bring your personality into play, and put yourself, not just your essay, up for judgment. You will be judged harshly.

Pretentious language asks to be shot down; pretentious langauge used incorrectly begs to be shot down.

Oh, the word "sesquipedalian"? One of my favorites— look it up.

Skip the Wise Guy Asides

These are the clever little commentaries students tack alongside their essays: political observations, irrelevant psychological remarks about people discussed in the essay, flash insights about life. The worst offenders offer tasteless jokes that aren't funny.

You will have plenty of opportunity to demonstrate your wit. On exams, stick to answering the questions.

Don't Overwrite

You've answered the question sufficiently but have time left and think you might as well write more. Control yourself. Writing more than required can jeopardize your grade in a number of ways.

- Remember: grading essays is a chore, and the more you write, the longer it takes to complete this chore. The annoyance could hurt your grade.
- You risk straying and saying something false, turning what was otherwise an outstanding essay into a mediocre essay. If the answer is X and you write X plus Y, and Y is false, then your essay as a whole is no longer true and you won't get the A.
- Even if your additional comments aren't false, they can water down your essay with drivel. When you add material, you run the risk of meandering. No padding by adding.

Don't Underwrite Either

Essay question: "Write what you know about the causes of the Battle of Hastings."

Student writes in his blue book the word "Nothing" and then demands an A on the grounds that he fully answered the question.

Another oft-repeated story tells of the philosophy final

whose question was the one word: "Why?" One student wrote, "Why not?" and received an A.

In the real world, your answer will need many more words to get the A. For even if you have done a magnificent job of capturing the answer in a few succinct words, your professor, rushing through the tens of essays, might not recognize your small gem of an answer.

Professors balk at giving a student an A for an essay of twenty words when they have just given a B+ to an essay of two hundred words. They will tell you that length doesn't count and that if you can say it in twenty-five words or less, all the better. Malarkey—length counts! Keep it lean and mean but not a skeleton.

TROUBLESHOOTING

Faking It

I wish it weren't so. I wish that essays were judged only on their merits and that students who rely on bull never get by. I also wish that war and poverty were permanently eradicated, that Michelle Pfeiffer had a crush on me, that I played the piano as well as Vladimir Horowitz, and that I could throw a ninety-five-mile-an-hour fastball. It ain't gonna happen. (Though maybe if Michelle met me . . .)

Making yourself sound more knowledgeable than you are is a talent that is natural to some but can be learned by all.

Some professors are more open to artful bulling than others. I remember how my own dependence on this ability got me through an art history class. I attended the class maybe twice all term (this isn't noted with bravado—it was stupid), having spent the bulk of the term in the student building, playing chess, talking politics, and socializing. I was a philosophy major and my art history teacher, lucky for me, fancied himself a serious thinker interested in "deeper meanings" of art. On the final, of course, we were asked to discuss the paintings and sculptures shown on slides. I was majestic. I couldn't identify a single work of art (never having seen them before), but I dished out the deeper meanings, the ontological angst, the tensions, the dynamism, buzzwords exploding in droves. I didn't ace the class, but I did get a B.

I tried the same gambit in a child psychology class, a course I considered even more ripe for plucking with the gift of gab. I managed a C only because I was familiar with some of the material.

Faking it is an emergency measure, not standard procedure. With that in mind, here are some tips on faking it through your essay.

If you can't be specific, generalize to the next level.

You aren't sure when Isaac Newton was born so you take a shot and write, "Newton was born in 1695." This is not a wise move, especially since Newton was born in 1642. But you don't know when he was born so what should you write? Try "Newton was born in the mid-seventeenth century." You aren't sure of the century? Try "several hundred years ago." The principle here is be as specific as you can, safely.

Write what you know.

You look at the essay question and it dawns on you with frightening clarity that you don't know this stuff at all. Panic begins to set in.

In these situations, test-wise students write what they know. We're assuming here that you do have a general knowledge of the course, and did study, perhaps even wrote out a sample essay—but studied the wrong article or the wrong topics.

Many essay questions have phrases that allow various interpretations. You will, of course, read the question so that, with clever splicing, you can haul in the stuff you know and write a full-fledged essay.

Most professors, while annoyed that you failed to answer the question directly, will also notice the superb essay you did write on a closely related matter. You will lose points for not answering the question directly, but your well-written essay will salvage some credit for your essay.

This advice is useless if today is the first time you've come to class and you know *nothing* about the subject or anything close to the subject. In that case, preserve your dignity and don't answer the question at all.

You Are Running Out of Time

You're steaming along on the last essay of the exam, writing like the blazes, when the instructor announces that you have three minutes left, so please start wrapping it up. You have exhausted too much time writing everything you knew about the universe in the previous essay and haven't enough time for this last essay. But you do know the answer. You have the facts but not the time.

Say it. Write, right there in your test booklet, that you've run out of time and cannot answer this essay as fully as intended. *Instead you will write a detailed outline of what you would have written had you more time.*

And that's what you do. You include a well-developed outline of your intended essay. This may not serve as a substitution for a fully written essay, but it will preserve a decent grade.

TAKE-HOME EXAMS

Take-home exams are strange animals grazing in the valley between essay exams and term papers. The problem with take-home exams is that expectations are unclear, both on the part of the professor and the student. How much can you quote from books? How much original work is necessary? Do "test conditions" apply?

Take-home exams are almost never short-answer tests—even the most trusting professor expects students to complete the exams with help from books and notes. Instead, professors try to devise take-home questions that require ingenuity and work. The students' answers should more closely resemble, in execution and quality, a mini-term paper.

In writing your take-home exam, don't copy from the class textbook; if you do, make sure to flag the passage with quotes. When you lift from the textbook, you will find yourself in the company of others in your class—none of you will get an A.

Treat the take-home much as you would a small term paper. Don't just sit down and write an essay as you would on an exam in class; think a lot longer about the answer. And as with term papers, type your take-home exams and hand in a professional-looking test.

Another variant of the take-home exam is the test consisting of questions which have been given to you beforehand. Here too, the A paper will have to rise to a higher standard than the standard in-class essay test. Analysis counts for more than memorization, and careless mistakes are judged less excusable. You should, of course, write out—in detail—the complete answer the night before.

MAKE-UP EXAMS

Avoid make-up exams if you can; they are bad news for both students and professors. Not surprisingly, some professors refuse to give make-up exams during the term, though if a student missed a final exam due to a genuine emergency, there isn't much alternative but to administer a make-up test.

Few professors are going to give you the same test they gave the rest of the class since they assume you have already discussed the test in depth with your classmates. This means they will have to construct a new test, and that is a big-time, unwelcome bother. True, it isn't your fault (you didn't choose to have that mad driver ram his car into yours as you drove to the test), but the nuisance of making up a new test is, nonetheless, directly attributable to you.

Most important, expect a more difficult exam than the one your class received. Expect, too, more stringent grading. You are working with a handicap—your professor's irritation—and you will have to perform unusually well to get the A. The solution? Watch out for mad drivers and make a heroic effort to get to the test on its scheduled day.

Short-Answer Tests

A man with one watch knows the time, a man with two isn't sure.

—CHINESE PROVERB

I used to be indecisive but now I'm not so sure.

—GRAFFITI

A fellow sits in the back of the room at the LSAT exam, rolling dice on his desk. He checks the dice and fills in the appropriate circle on the multiple choice answer sheet. The proctor announces that the test is over in ten minutes and suggests that everyone review his answers. So the guy frantically starts tossing his dice to check his answers.

THE MULTIPLE CHOICE TEST

Strategy

I don't suppose you have ever invented a multiple choice test, but I recommend that you try it. You will discover how difficult it is to make up *any* multiple choice test and how *very* difficult it is to make up a good one. This is why professors borrow multiple choice test questions from books, lectures, and other tests. (Creating a multiple choice test, by the way, is an excellent way to study: it is a wonderful way to review details and important distinctions. If you have a study partner, try composing tests for each other.)

To answer multiple choice tests successfully, you need to understand how they are devised. The hardest part to developing multiple choice exams is coming up with five reasonable choices for each question. You can use this difficulty to your benefit, as we shall soon see. Another important feature of multiple choice tests is your professor's desire to trick you—or, at a minimum, to make you sweat a bit. If you are astute, you can turn this, too, to your advantage.

Get an Overview of the Exam before Writing

Instructions are especially important on multiple choice tests so pay careful attention to them. Professors invent uncommon directions such as asking for "two plausible choices" instead of one, or asking that you write your answers on the question sheet or on the back of the test booklet.

If there's a sample problem, study it carefully. Sample problems indicate whether the questions are straightforward or subtle and the kind of response expected of you.

Finally, skim all the question stems, the first part of the question, but not all the possible choices—you don't have time to read them all. This way you'll have an idea of the difficulty of the exam and pace yourself accordingly. You'll also note which later questions might contain suggestions for answering earlier questions.

Think of an Answer before You Read the Choices

After you read the question, take a moment to answer it to yourself, and then look at the choices. If one of the choices is the same as your proposed answer, give that choice serious consideration. Proposing an answer before you read the choices also helps you get in tune with the style and thinking of the test maker, and that, too, will speed you toward the correct answer.

Read Every Choice

Test makers try to put at least two plausible answers in every question, and when they succeed, the answers are as confusingly similar as identical twins. Choice "b" sounds like the right answer, but choice "d," when you get to it, sounds even more like the right answer. Read all the choices before you make your selection.

Watch Out for Dirty Tricks

Professors have two reasons for including similar choices on a multiple choice test: one is to see if you really have the idea down cold, and the other is to fool you. Other forms of chicanery in multiple choice tests are sneaky qualifying phrases, double negatives, and sleights of language. When you complain about this later on, the professor will righteously intone, "Had you read the question more carefully, you would have noticed that it specifically says. . . ." Why professors revel in these ruses has more to do with their own insecurity or misplaced sense of play than with a desire to test your knowledge.

Can you tell if your professor falls into this category of tricksters? Not easily; even the softies enjoy reminding you of their authority by hitting you with a trick question, while the stern professors might stick to precise, no-nonsense questions. The upshot is, be on your guard. As the man said, "Trust everyone, but cut the deck."

INTELLIGENT GUESSING

College tests rarely deduct points for wrong answers, so don't leave any multiple choice blank. But wild guessing is only a last resort. You can guess intelligently and increase the probability of guessing correctly. To make intelligent conjectures on multiple choice tests, you need to recall the strategic underpinning suggested at the outset: understand how multiple choice tests are constructed.

Most instructors are delighted if they can formulate four solid, plausible answers; three reasonable choices and one only marginally reasonable choice is usually good enough. This means that you can discard one of the choices with no trouble and a second choice with not much more difficulty. Now, you have a one-out-of-three chance of getting the right answer with a random guess. If you are on sure grounds for most of the test and have close to a 33 percent chance on the other, weaker questions, you are within range of a respectable grade.

You can use other probabilities to your advantage. Be aware, and beware: The tips that follow are bracketed with the word "generally" or "most often." *They are not meant to apply in every case.* Note, too, that wily professors will deliberately try to entrap you by crafting their answers to go against expectations.

With these warnings in place, let's look at a few tips for selective guessing.

Grammatical Errors Occur More Often in Wrong Answers

There are fewer ways to say what you want to say than not to say what you want to say. To put this point another way: A mistake is more likely to make a true sentence false than a false sentence true. This is why grammatical errors are more likely to show up in the wrong choices than the correct choice. The test maker, attending to the correct answer, gives it the most attention of all the choices. The wrong answers get comparably less attention, and that's where you will find the preponderance of mistakes of gender, tense, and number.

But remember, like bad offspring in the best of families, typos and grammatical mistakes occur in the best of answers as well.

One Answer in a Pair of Opposites Is Often the Correct Choice

If the choices include two answers that are the opposite of each other, there's a good chance that one of them is the correct answer. It is difficult to invent two choices, both of which are plausible answers, relevant to the question, contradictory to each other, and false; it is much easier to devise contradictory sentences which meet these requirements if one is true and the other false. Attend to these opposite pair choices; the answer may well lurk there.

Be Wary of Absolutes

Be on the lookout for such words as "never," "always," "none," "all." I wouldn't assert with certainty that words with absolutes are only used in incorrect choices, but they most often are.

Test makers shy from using absolute terms in the correct answer because they know that few things in this world are unconditional. I play it safe by using such phrases as "tends to," "most, if not all," "generally," and other qualifiers that allow for the stray exception.

I also "tend" to shun absolutes to avoid confrontations with the perennial wise-guy student. When the correct answer asserts that something is always or never the case, some student-turned-constitutional-lawyer is sure to argue for a technicality which, he claims, renders my absolute incorrect. This student's effort is a desperate and unsupportable ploy, but it's also a nuisance I can do without.

STRATEGIC GUESSING

Stay with One Letter Throughout or Skip Around?

Students have long been perplexed by this dilemma. Suppose you are reduced to random guessing; should you go with the same letter straight down the line? Are you better off spreading out your choices on the assumption that your professor wants to mix up the order of correct answers? When you have a row of five "c"s, and haven't seen a "d" yet, it's natural to get a little nervous.

If the order of answers were truly random, as they are

in most standardized tests, it wouldn't make a difference how you choose your answers; you have the same probability of getting a twenty (assuming five choices per question) whether you use only one letter or skip around.

But few professors structure tests that are genuinely random. (Word processing is making randomization easier; you can throw a dice, say, and then with cut and paste editing, move your answers to correspond to the toss.) Professors try to get their answers to have a random pattern, and they succeed well enough but not perfectly. For example, I would bet (but not the whole farm) that choice "e" is less often correct than other letters. At the same time, instructors usually try to include every letter as the correct answer at least once, whereas a pure randomizing machine has no such psychological inclination.

What follows from all this? Not very much. If you answer every question with the same letter, you probably will avoid a zero—that's not much to celebrate about. When you see too many "d"s in a row, you itch to switch to another letter, but that might be unadvisable. Perhaps an earlier "d" choice was wrong or perhaps your professor has a perverse love of the letter "d."

It's like betting at the track. The race might be fixed, but as long as you don't know *how*, you bet as you would if it wasn't fixed. Your professor tries, if only semiconsciously, to make his sequence of correct answers random, but as long as you don't know what that process is, your guesses are as good as mine.

The conclusion? Don't bother looking for patterns.

Should You Change Your Answers?

"Stick to your first choice," goes the advice, "because your first intuition is your best." It's widespread advice and widely believed. It is also a myth.

You remember the times you changed your choice from the right answer to the wrong ones, but you forget the times you changed from the wrong answers to the right ones: our collisions stand out far more than our near-misses.

I have never seen, though not for lack of searching, any conclusive evidence to support the recommendation not to alter your first choice when you think you should. In fact, from my own limited, informal survey of crossed-out answers, the opposite seems the case: answers changed upon reflection are correct more often than the initial answer. So even if you believe in love at first sight, don't believe in truth at first sight. If, upon reconsideration, you prefer a different answer than your original choice, go with your later judgment.

Is That an "A" or a "D"? Don't Fudge

To answer a multiple choice test you only have to know the first five letters of the alphabet. College students know these letters so well they can write them with great variety. They can craft a lowercase "a" that looks remarkably similar to a lowercase "d," or drop the thinnest line across their "c" to transform it (maybe) into an "e."

The point of all this ambiguity is to write the letter unclearly in the hope that the grader will read the letter as the correct answer.

It doesn't work. Not only doesn't it work, you can lose points this way. A "c" with a line across it doesn't look either like a "c" or an "e"; it looks like a "c" with a line across it. Your professor will read it as a "c," or an "e," or he might read it as a concoction letter designed to fool him. You are telegraphing the fact that you aren't sure about the answer.

When you can't decide between two letters, guess—this

way you have a fifty-fifty chance of being right. An equivocal letter, on the other hand, encourages a third possible reading: a "nonletter" that will be marked as incorrect.

If, on the other hand, you want to *avoid* ambiguity and you are afraid, say, that your "a" will be read as a "d," you can write out a key word from the correct choice. But otherwise, and this means just about always, write only the letter of the correct answer, not the words. Writing out the answer in words is an enormous, senseless, though not uncommon, waste of time.

SHORT-ANSWER BRIEFS: DESCRIBE, IDENTIFY, OR DISCUSS

The most common form of short-answer tests in college (along with the true/false and multiple choice tests) are exams that ask you to "briefly" define, explain, analyze, or discuss a term or concept.

What Counts as "Briefly"?

Length is always a problem on these sorts of tests. How much to write? Although professors have different ideas about what qualifies as adequate, a few guidelines are in order.

Unlike essay exams which aren't always read in full, short answers are. Write too little and your omissions demand attention. A three-word answer might suffice for a fill-in-the-blank quiz but not for one that asks for a brief discussion; three words is a grunt, not an analysis.

The more subtle danger is overwriting. You've answered the question but proceed to say more. Hold on: If it takes three sentences to answer the question, the fourth sentence is an invitation for a penalty. The more you write, the greater the chance of writing something wrong, or saying something right in the wrong way, which is much the same. Leave well enough alone.

Faking It on the Short Answers

Faking it on short-answer tests is more difficult than on an essay test. On essay tests, if you know a related issue you can find a connection, write what you know, and garner some points. You don't have this luxury in short-answer tests where your attempt to dodge the question is noticed immediately.

Do write something if you have a shot at the answer or even part of the answer. Particularly in math exams or science tests, show some work so that a sympathetic grader will have some basis to give you partial credit.

But if you haven't the faintest idea about the question, leave it blank. I have exhorted you to answer every question, but this is the one exception. Individual questions on short-answer tests are not worth that many points and you can afford not getting the credit for the question. When you write any old gibberish you lose your credibility, and that will cost you points on your other answers.

The Term Paper

Your manuscript is both good and original; but
the part that is good is not original, and the part
that is original is not good.

—SAMUEL JOHNSON

What do you do if you can't think of a topic?

Are you better off with a safe subject or something original?

Do all those rules about footnotes and bibliography count in determining your grade?

I assign a paper and my students form a beeline to my office. Can I suggest a topic? How long does it have to be? When is it due? Can the student include his own opinion?

Writing a term paper is, for good reason, a major college worry. **You *must* learn how to write term papers to do well in many of your classes.**

Good papers don't take longer to research than bad papers; good papers don't take longer to write than bad ones; and good papers might not even have superior content. What distinguishes the good paper from the bad one is better structure and the *look* of a serious piece of work.

The subjective element is especially pivotal in grading papers. The same paper that gets an A with one professor can get a C with another. A good part of the grade depends on form and style: the organization of data and arguments, the appearance of sophistication. Students who get A's on their papers know what an A presentation looks like. You have to learn it, too.

We can divide our guided tour of term papers into questions of "software" and "hardware." Software issues include how to choose a topic, gather and organize information, and develop a winning style. Hardware questions involve the "look" of the term paper.

SOFTWARE

Step One: Stay Cool

Remember those grade-school book reports on *Death Be Not Proud* and *Anne Frank: The Diary of a Young Girl*? You managed decent book reports back then without undergoing trauma. In high school you had to do a report on the causes of WWI or a study on Saturn, so you pieced together a few articles from a couple of encyclopedias. These assignments were less specific than the grade-school reports and required more of your own input, but you survived them as well. College term papers require even more of a personal contribution, but it's more of the same. Don't get overwhelmed—you'll do fine once again.

Step Two: Choose a Topic You Care About

You'll run into two groups of professors. Group one assigns you a very specific topic. Group two is vague: "Do something related to the subject matter." Group two is much larger than group one.

Your choice of topic is a critical decision, so get it right.

It's *essential* that you pick a topic not because you think your professor cares about it, not because you think you *should* care about it, but because you *do* care about it. Even if your professor assigns you a topic, use your inventiveness to work up enthusiasm for the project.

I make a big deal about this requirement. Before students decide on a term paper topic, they must explain why they want to spend time on that particular issue. "It sounds interesting" doesn't cut it. They have to convince me that the issue challenges them. Too often I see students choose a term paper topic in which they have no interest but think will be easy, only to find themselves stuck with a project they hate. Invariably, they do a poor job.

You could be concerned with many more issues than you imagine. Your interests could include the economic structure of developing nations in Africa. You could be curious about the power of labor unions during the Depression. You may want to analyze Melville's influence on contemporary literature. As H. L. Mencken remarked, "There are no dull subjects. There are only dull writers." People spend their whole lives on some pretty way-out subjects; you can maintain an interest in these subjects for a couple of months.

Having a personal interest in the topic offers two significant benefits.

- **It's easier to do the work.** Research and writing require an intense effort but it's a lot less agonizing if you care about the project.
- **You're more likely to be intellectually honest.** As we will soon see, A papers always present both sides of an argument. You'll be fair if you care.

Step Three: Come Up with an Original Topic

Please, please, please. Another paper on euthanasia will drive me to try it on myself. (On the other hand, a superb paper on youth in Asia . . .)

Professors teach the same courses year in, year out, so it's not surprising that they get repeat topics for term papers. What is fresh for the student is stale for the professor. If you choose a banal topic, you can assume that your professor has already read hundreds of student papers on the subject. Presumably, a few of those papers were better than yours. Your professor will remember how well the subject can be discussed, and grade your paper against that exemplary standard.

A creative topic, on the other hand, is much more fun to read. You'll get points just for being innovative. But be careful: originality isn't enough; the topic must have substance, too. A paper on male chauvinism in *Batman* sounds promising, but is there a genuine term paper here? Stray, but stay within the guidelines.

Step Four: Visit the Library

It's wonderful that the Civil War fascinates you, but unless you're prepared to write seventeen volumes on the subject, the origins of the Civil War is a tad too broad for a term paper. On the other hand, the growth rate of Stonewall Jackson's beard is a tad too narrow. Try something in-between.

How much has been written on the topic? Too much? Too little? Is the information accessible?

Before you commit to a subject, check out its suitability at the library. If the scope of your paper is so wide that you find a dozen books devoted to it, back off—you're biting off too much. A manageable topic is discussed in a few chapters in a few books, and in several journal articles.

Step Five: The Directory Shortcut Stratagem

What if you can't think of a decent topic? What if you're not sure whether your topic is any good?

Welcome to the secret world of the directory. A treasure for term papers awaits you.

Every discipline has its own directory. These directories—sometimes called reviews or annuals—are listings of all the articles that have been published in the respective fields. Every college library has a directory of this kind for nearly every subject: psychology, American history, philosophy, art, economics, et cetera. More than just listings, these directories also contain short summaries of each listed article. Directories are usually issued four times a year, and go back for decades.

Subject directories are a reservoir for paper topics. Here, you can find out which are the field's hot topics, what is ignored, what is controversial, how professionals title their papers, and where to find what you need once you've settled on a subject.

Step Six: Discuss Your Topic with Your Teacher

The first time most professors learn about your paper is when they grade it. From your perspective, this is very unadvisable.

Whether or not it's required, discuss your paper topic with your teacher. This accomplishes several purposes.

- **No surprises.** You won't wait until the end of the term and three months of excruciating work to find out that your topic is unacceptable.
- **Your professor gets involved with your project.** He'll happily spout his opinion, gossip about people in his field and ridicule their ideas. He'll recommend books and articles, and a few of these recommendations might help. He'll enjoy the opportunity to play mentor and may reward you with a better grade.
- **You gauge your professor's reactions.** You want to know as early as possible if he thinks your point of view is totally out to lunch.

Step Seven: Formulate a Core Question

Whether you are doing a two-page paper or a doctoral thesis, step seven is crucial. **Your project should be driven by a single, clearly stated question.**

A core question is important for legal briefs, business plans, medical diagnoses, and most other writing projects. It is *vital* for term papers and theses. Ask yourself: "What is the essential issue here? What is the fundamental problem I'm trying to solve?" If you don't have an interesting question, you won't have an interesting answer.

You should be able to state the basic issue in the proverbial twenty-five words or less. The question needn't appear in the title, but you should state it early in your paper; this gives the reader a clear idea about where you intend to lead him.

If you can't formulate the problem clearly, your paper will be all over the place. A term paper "about French Impressionism" leaves no impression at all, and a paper "on Cezanne" isn't much more in season. A paper that addresses the question "What was Cezanne's approach to perspective in drawing?" begins to have some direction.

A central question keeps your paper on track and helps you read and write with a focus. It's impossible to overstate the usefulness of this device.

Step Eight: Back to the Directory

After you've decided on a topic, go back to the directory of articles we discussed above. Dig in. You're going to shine.

Most college students, especially during the first terms of college, don't have a clue as to what a professional article looks like. Why should they? They didn't spend their adolescence hiding under the blankets sneaking peeks at sociology journals.

But journal articles are precisely what your sociology professor reads and writes. Because younger faculty need to publish articles to get ahead in their field, they, in particular, keep up with the academic literature. These journal publications are what professors consider standard; your term paper looks like a high school composition in comparison.

These journals aren't state secrets. You too can discover the "professional" format in sociology, history, political science . . . in every college subject. Thanks to the directory.

First, look up your professor's name. Go back a couple of years. If she's published anything, look it up. You don't have to actually read the article, but do peruse it. You'll discover a great deal about your teacher's interests, writing style, and lots of subjective qualities that are hard to specify. It's all useful information.

Discuss your professor's work in your paper, but only if it's relevant. Don't mention your professor's article on recent Peruvian foreign policy if your paper is about the Republican party in the Sun Belt states—you don't want to be an obvious brownnose. But if appropriate, incorporate your professor's written work into your paper. Tell her that in the course of your research you came across her paper and found it most interesting. It's flattery all right, but it's flattery that works.

Pay attention to the style of these journal articles. Social science articles aren't written in the same format as articles in the humanities, both of which differ from articles in the sciences. For example, publications in most of the social sciences include bibliographies in the body of the text, while humanities articles often do not.

To help you find what you need, talk to the reference librarians. Don't be shy about asking for their assistance; it's what they do for a living and your tuition helps pay their salaries.

Step Nine: Write before You Are Ready to Write

Writing not only organizes your thinking, it organizes your reading. When you just research, you pile up mounds of scattered and useless information, thinking everything might find its way into your paper. But when you put ideas to paper you start reading with direction. Although you still zig and zag over the course of your project, at least you are not all over the map. Students who suffer through the horrors of writing a thesis learn this eventually, although usually too late.

Step Ten: Use Secondary Sources

If you are having difficulty with the primary material, avail yourself of secondary material. Check out reviews of the books you're analyzing. Look at other textbooks, anthologies, and even encyclopedia articles. First, try to read the primary material you are working on, the book, say, that your paper is about, and then have a look at secondary material, other books and articles which discuss that book. When you are finished researching the secondary sources, return to the primary material. Your paper, enriched by these other authors, will now read as well-founded analysis.

Step Eleven: Present the Other Side

As we noted in our discussion of essay exams, a common defect of college papers is the failure to state both sides of an issue.

In the worst case, the student simply neglects to present the opposing viewpoint. Close behind is the paper that presents the opposition as blathering idiots. Remember, if your opponent is a fool, then you've only succeeded in defeating a fool (if the opposing point of view is that nonsensical, it's not worth arguing about in the first place). Provocative controversies have plausible arguments on both sides, and until you've satisfactorily presented the other side's reasoning, you haven't demonstrated the superiority of your own point of view.

Don't be stingy. Make the case for the opposition as strong as you can. You might even persuade yourself that you need to modify your original position . . . or abandon it completely. Such is the price of intellectual honesty.

Put more emphatically: **A careful presentation of both sides of an issue—and that alone—assures you of a high grade.**

Step Twelve: Don't Turn Your Term Paper into an Autobiography

Even your unsubstantiated beliefs matter to you. After all, unsupported or not, they are your beliefs. Transforming term papers into extended diaries is a common student conceit; these students are enamored of their opinions and think such meanderings form an adequate substitute for research. To your professor, your unfounded ideas are insignificant, and if they comprise the main ingredient of your paper, you can expect a low grade.

If you insist on including your "feelings" and "opinions" in your papers, make sure to buttress them with arguments and evidence.

Step Thirteen: Edit, Edit, and When You Are Finished Editing, Edit Again

According to Mark Twain, "Writers should strike out every third word on principle; you have no idea what vigor it adds to your style."

Do you want your professor to take your term paper seriously? Then *you* had better take it seriously. If the first draft and the final version of your paper are identical—and so often students only bother with one version—don't expect your paper to get any respect. Revise your paper—repeatedly.

Your most important editing tool is the scissors. Fine tuning by fine pruning.

The standard advice when packing for a trip is to put back half of the clothes you think you'll need and then start selecting from the remaining half. Similarly, you can dump half of what you wrote and improve your paper in the process.

Have you gotten rid of repetitions and cut away the fat?

Does your paper say what you want it to say . . . and no more? Then put it away for a while. You need distance. At minimum, let it rest overnight. You'll read it later with fresh eyes and see things you can't believe were there— or won't see things you can't believe you left out.

Then give the paper to a friend for comments.

David Oglivy, advertising guru of his generation and a man renowned for his writing skills, sent drafts of his more important memos to his colleagues with one word written on them: "Improve."

Don't argue; don't get defensive. If your friend's suggestions are helpful, use them. If not, thank him and move on.

Step Fourteen: Submit a Draft or Outline to Your Professor

The usual term paper procedure is as follows: the professor gives the class a deadline for paper submissions, and you wait until three days before the deadline to write the bloody thing. By that time, you're so crazed and busy that you're delighted just to get the paper done. You can't be bothered with questions of quality at this point.

Here's a better idea.

Ask your professor if she "would be so kind" (or words to that effect) as to read an early draft of your paper. If the best you can muster is an outline, ask her to read that. Explain that you want assurance that you are on the right track and would greatly benefit from her feedback.

Most professors will comply. They intensely dislike grading exams and papers, but you aren't asking them to do any grading; you just want some professional advice. How can they refuse?

You will get confirmation, encouragement, and guidance. And, best of all, an early submission insures that you will get the paper done on time.

HARDWARE

I've got sixty-three term papers stacked on my desk waiting to be graded. I'd rather be watching a ball game. I'd rather be reading a mystery. I'd even rather be reading an article in a philosophy journal. This isn't fun, but it must get done.

I apprehensively look at the stack. Most seem all right: reasonable number of pages, typed, and, in a few instances, bound. Several papers look sorry. One is written on paper ripped from a spiral notebook, another is smudged, still another smells of cheap perfume and has a ribbon on it.

The uninviting papers I put on the bottom. These will have to go the extra mile to get the A. By the time I get to them I'd even rather do the dishes.

The appearance of your paper counts a great deal. Let's review some of the features of a good-looking paper.

How Long Should the Paper Be?

The most frequent question I'm asked as soon as I assign a term paper is "How many pages do you require?"

Don't join the chorus. Asking the question makes you seem "studenty" and not concerned with serious matters. You'll get a shrug that says your paper should be as long as needed.

Contrary to legend, professors don't grade papers on the basis of weight, but two pages just isn't enough for a course term paper. Obviously, no one expects a forty-page tome either. Try for something in the middle.

Technical Matters Matter

Packaging counts. The reaction to a messy paper is natural: If the student doesn't have pride in his work, the professor will have even less respect for it. To ensure that A, make sure that your paper meets all the stationery requirements: typed on decent typing paper, stapled or paper-clipped, paginated. This should be obvious, but judging from the scruffy papers I still get every term, it's worth emphasizing once again.

You also have to take care of the technical aspects of the paper, such as footnotes and bibliography: what goes first, author or book, the difference between *ibid* and *op cit*, and other regulations of style. Consult your handbook to learn how to format a research paper correctly. If you don't have the right guidebook on your desk, you'll find what you need in the library.

Your professor might be among those who are sticklers about proper form. It pays to get it right.

Type

A handwritten paper begs for a low grade.

Handwritten papers are generally unacceptable, so this reminder is unnecessary for most of you. But even if your professor will accept handwritten papers, type yours. **This rule is an absolute: Never submit a handwritten paper.**

If you can't type, learn how to type. If you can't learn how to type, get a girlfriend or boyfriend who can. If all else fails, pay to have your paper typed. All college newspapers advertise typists looking for work. These are usually fellow students and they aren't expensive; if you can't afford their services, work out a creative barter arrangement.

The Wonderful World of Word Processing

Ask me about word processing and I'll gush like a crusader. For years I resisted computers. "Too cold for my taste," I righteously concluded. "Hey, Tolstoy wrote *War and Peace* without word processing and did pretty well."

Well, maybe if Tolstoy had used a word processor, *War and Peace* wouldn't be so darn long. In my case, I'm sure had I started using a word processor earlier, I would have written five times as much as I did.

If you already use a computer for writing, you know its advantages. If you don't, listen up.

Word processing is to typing as typing is to writing by hand. With a word processor, you not only write faster and easier, but you also write better. Writing well is partly a function of when you give up. At some point you just throw up your hands with an exasperated, "Okay, enough." As the poets say, "You don't finish a poem, you abandon it."

Word processing emancipates you from a premature desire to abandon your work. When you're typing, you allow a passable but uninspired phrase to remain in your text because it's just not worth the hassle of retyping a whole page. With a word processing program you can alter or eliminate the offending words in a second or two.

For writing term papers, the word processor is magic. Essential magic.

- **You organize effectively.** Gone are the scraps of paper, dislocated chapter fragments, notes strewn all over your room. All the scattered information is neatly arranged in your computer, classified, and easily accessible.
- **Outlining is easy.** Most word processing programs come with built-in, easy-to-use outline features.
- **You can say bye-bye to spelling mistakes and typos.** A spell check takes care of that. Fancier grammar programs will even flag your grammatical errors. Thesaurus programs are available too, offering instant erudition.

Another advantage of word processors is that by storing your work on a disk you always have a copy of it.

The price of computers is dwindling, as is the price of word processing programs that run on these computers. If you can't afford a computer, check out the new typewriter/word processing machines; this will suffice if all you need is a writing machine.

If you can't afford a typewriter/word processor either, use the computer facilities at school. Most colleges provide students with the use of a computer terminal, so find out about the computer services available to you.

Keep a Copy of Your Paper

Professors misplace papers. They can misplace your paper and claim they never got it. It's not an uncommon problem—and it's your problem: you will probably have to resubmit the paper.

Make copies not only of the final version but of every draft along the way. This way, even if you haven't stored the paper in your computer as suggested above, you won't have to reinvent a lost draft the week before the deadline.

It's another instance of "better safe than very sorry."

On Writing

I have nothing but contempt for anyone who can spell a word only one way.

—THOMAS JEFFERSON

A woman on a motorcycle crosses the Mexican border twice a week. She always carries a sack. "What do you have in there?" the border guards ask each time she crosses. "Potatoes," the woman says. Finally, the guards demand to have a look. Sure enough the sack contains potatoes.

On the other side of the border, the woman's friend asks her what's really going on. "I'm smuggling," says the woman. "Smuggling what?" asks the friend. "Motorcycles," answers the woman.

How you deliver determines *what* you deliver or, as the more common phrase has it, "the medium is the message." In college, the student's central medium is the written word. Writing is so crucial to good grades in school that it deserves its own little chapter.

The fact that you're a computer science major or plan to be an astrophysicist doesn't exempt you from the need to write well; even the elephant trainer has to write letters to moving companies. The deterioration in the writing ability of all segments of our population means that the businessperson, and any other professional who writes well, has a significant advantage over his competitors.

In college the need for writing is, in any case, incontrovertible. You will have to write often, so get used to it . . . and get good at it.

WRITE RIGHT

What do you need to do to improve your writing? Just two things:

- read a lot; and
- write a lot.

Simple, isn't it? It is simple if you already have the basics in hand. If you don't, you'll need some help.

Every college offers remedial writing programs. You have a choice: either yield to your embarrassment and shy away from help, or overcome your pride and get the assistance you need. The former route leads to poor grades, the latter route to better grades. I've intentionally set up this dilemma with lopsided results—false self-esteem can be very costly here.

A writing course will accentuate your writing difficulties: poor sentence construction, weaknesses in grammar, mistakes of usage. Diagnosis is half the cure. The best part of these classes is that they have you writing, and as in every skill from acrobatics and bowling to yodelling and zebra hunting, practice is the key to learning.

YOUR REFERENCE LIBRARY

The violinist searches for the best available strings, and the baseball player insists on the bat that suits him best. In every human endeavor, the better the tools, the better the product.

You are students, not professional writers (yet), and you don't need a writer's comprehensive reference library. But you will do more writing than most people on this planet and will need adequate equipment to do your job well. This equipment, by the way, is extremely cost-effective; it is relatively inexpensive and lasts a lifetime. Here is the basic gear:

A Decent Dictionary

"Decent" excludes those $1.95 school paperbacks with a few hundred words in bold print. You will keep your dictionary for many years so invest in a hefty, respectable edition. Take the time to learn how your dictionary is organized and what the abbreviations mean. You'll be surprised by the range of interesting information contained in a good dictionary.

There are several excellent dictionaries to choose from. The following are among the good choices: *Webster's New Collegiate Dictionary* (Springfield: Merriam-Webster Inc.), *American Heritage Dictionary* (New York: Harper & Row), *Random House College Dictionary* (New York: Random House).

A Grammar/Usage Book

The word "grammar" makes people break out in ugly hives, but with the right attitude you can turn grammar from foe to friend. The trick is to step back and try to understand the logic behind all the rules and the illogic behind the thousands of exceptions to these rules.

Does the exclamation mark go inside or outside the quotation marks? Is that *affect* or *effect?* Is it, "Everyone got what they deserve," or, "Everyone got what he deserves"? When these posers emerge, look up the answers in your trusty handbook; after a while you'll be checking less and less as you learn more and more.

Many comprehensive, easy-to-read grammar books are available. These books don't always have the word "grammar" in the title. Some are called handbooks, manuals, basic English, and the like. Pick up a copy of the slim classic *The Elements of Style*, by Strunk and White, for a leading example of the genre.

A Style Book for Papers

How do you write a bibliography? What's the deal with footnotes? What comes first, author or book title? What does *op. cit.* mean, and when do I use *ibid.*? A style book has the answers as do some of the better handbooks.

A popular standard in this category is *The Student Guide for Writing College Papers*, by Kate L. Turabian (Chicago: The University of Chicago Press).

A Thesaurus

What's another word for "synonymous"? With a thesaurus you can cheat along with the best. A thesaurus won't turn you into a James Joyce, but it will help you find the best words to say what you have to say. Ours is a language rich in nuance and an extensive thesaurus can upgrade your written presentation . . . and your grades.

Thesauri have various structures, so shop for the one that seems easiest to use. For the computer users among you, consider buying a thesaurus program. They are well worth the expense.

A Book on the Craft of Writing

These books don't address the details of grammar and usage but are devoted to the broader techniques of writing. Not only do these books provide tips on structuring, editing, revising, and other writing tactics, they also offer the inspiration you'll need when confronting major term papers and research assignments.

Outstanding books on writing abound, some written by writing teachers and others by well-known authors (one favorite is *On Writing Well*, by William Zinsser). The better ones are worth reading and belong on your permanent reference shelf.

An Almanac

Almanacs are a wonderful repository of useful and absolutely useless information. What's the name of the currency used in Indonesia? Who won the gold medal in the javelin throw in the 1956 Olympics? What is the largest dam in Africa? The details found in the Almanac will spice your writing and help your studies as well. Don't be surprised to find yourself dipping into this encyclopedia of facts with surprisingly regularity.

Almanacs (*World Books* and *Information Please* are other titles; they are all much the same) come out once a year. Save money and buy last year's issue. The fact that the Democratic candidate Winfield S. Hancock lost the 1880 presidential election didn't change over the past year and that's true of most of the information in the almanac. The only real difference is that this year's edition will cost you a lot more than the buck or two you will pay for last year's edition.

All of the books suggested above are available in your college library and some, such as the handbooks and books on writing, circulate. The early bird catches the book-worm. Get 'em while they're hot.

9

Get Smart

> An intellectual is someone who watches himself
> think.
>
> —ALBERT CAMUS

Will extracurricular activities hurt or help my grades?

How can I become better informed?

Will a term abroad make a difference to my grades?

To get better grades, it helps to be smart. Okay, you knew that, but did you know that you can *choose* to get smart?

A big part of the grade game is impressing your teacher in class, in his office, on exams and papers. Professors, like everyone else, assume a connection between smarts and good grades; if they think you're intelligent, they expect you to have done well on your exam and will grade your work accordingly. They'll give you the benefit of the doubt and read through your paper without stopping to look for errors.

Intelligence improves all facets of your schoolwork. Well-informed students are better at writing, drawing interesting connections, and making impressive allusions.

These abilities are especially useful when you are ill-prepared and need to wing an assignment. *To fake it well, you need intelligence—but you can't fake intelligence.*

Genuine intelligence requires a genuine commitment to learning.

THE FAME GAME

You had a terrible high-school education.

How do I know? Study after study, survey after survey, reaffirms the bad news: If you're a typical American high-school graduate, you got a bum deal. Among industrialized countries, Americans score among the lowest in general information, and the very lowest in the sciences, math, and geography. American kids' knowledge of current events and world politics is dismal.

If you think this doesn't apply to you, take this little test—but take it honestly.

Name two important living American painters. (Okay, name one—and Andy Warhol is dead.) Name a living writer who has won the Nobel Prize. I'll settle for any three serious writers (that means a cut above Robert Ludlum and Stephen King).

For extra points, name a classical musician. For a hundred points name a living composer of classical music. For a thousand points name an important living physicist. For a hundred thousand points, name an important living poet. For a million points, name an important historian. For a gazillion points, name a significant mathematician.

I play the Fame Game with almost all my classes (they are average or better-than-average college students), and the response is usually the same: few students can answer more than one of the above.

If you couldn't come up with any names, don't blame yourself. Who is famous in this country? Actors, athletes, and politicians (who are often the same people: a former president was an actor, and several presidential candidates are former athletes). Fame comes only to those who get on television, and that excludes most people doing significant, influential work.

The moral of this story is that if you are interested in what's going on in the world, you must dig deeper than the mass media. You need to expand your sources and find out the story underneath the story. Even what you learn in class isn't enough. You have to educate yourself.

Here are a few things you can do to help.

READ THE NEWSPAPER
EVERY DAY

Want to be smarter than most of your professors? Read the *New York Times* every day.

All right, the *Washington Post*. The point is to read a serious newspaper daily and yes, the *New York Times* is probably the best of all, and no, the *National Enquirer* does not qualify as a serious newspaper.

It's hard to overestimate the benefits of this ritual. As a result of this daily reading, your vocabulary improves, your grammar improves, your spelling improves, and your writing skills improve. And that's just for starters. You also learn about politics, geography, history, economics, science, art, and culture.

It takes time to get through the *Times*, even if you don't look up yesterday's weather in Helsinki. You don't have to read the paper cover to cover, but you should read most of the articles on the front page, a few other articles here and there, and scan all headlines. After a while, you'll be astonished at how much you've learned. Some years ago, I realized that if I read the obituary column every day, I'd eventually read about all the important people who die before I do.

Soon you will become addicted, a news junkie. You will still read other papers for other interests (the *New York Times* sports section lacks juice), but you'll crave the superior newspaper's hard news.

MAGAZINES

Start snooping around magazines. You know about *Time*, *Newsweek*, *Playboy*, *Vogue*, maybe *Esquire*, maybe *Elle*, definitely *People* and *Sports Illustrated*, and certainly a few more, but you may not yet have discovered the world of specialized magazines.

There's a magazine for every taste, for every hobby, for every political shrug, for every fleeting fantasy. There are lowbrow magazines and highbrow magazines, magazines to impress your dates with and magazines you still hide from your parents.

Start subscribing to magazines that respect what you want to become. Read magazines that esteem intelligence—whatever the subject or political stance. If your love is dance, film, politics, or literature, subscribe to a magazine in that field. It will deepen your interest at little expense. Magazine subscriptions are one of the best bargains in town, and because of your status as a student, publishers will quickly and forever badger you to buy their magazines at extremely reduced prices. Comply.

READ BOOKS

Books? You have enough, you say with a justified wave of the arm. Your fingertips are already calloused from balancing the tips of the nine textbooks you lug around campus, and you can do just fine, thank you very much, without reading another book "just for fun." Hey, if you managed to get through even half of your assignments, you wouldn't have any spare time for spare reading.

True, but then you don't spend the whole year in school. Add your summer vacation to your holiday vacations and your mid/tri-semester winter/spring breaks and then add the time you spend on the bus, at the laundromat, eating alone in the cafeteria, waiting for the bureaucrat at the bursar's office to lift her head, waiting for your date to show up, and you'll find lots of time to read.

Some of you do already read; most of you do not. According to a recent survey, only 20 percent of college students buy books other than textbooks.

Fiction Is for Real

What do college students read? Best sellers. I'm not sure why we should have expected otherwise, but the best-selling books on campus are much the same as those on the national best-seller list.

That's not good enough for you. *If you want to become educated, you need to develop taste.* And that means reading beyond the popular.

Thrillers and romances are fine afternoon-at-the-beach reading. If you read *Heart-throb III* or *The Born Again Bourne Conspiracy* you still get points because you are voluntarily reading a book, and that in itself sets you apart. But a reading diet based exclusively on such "mindless" diversion is as nourishing as eating exclusively at McDonald's (and as bland). Once you develop literary taste, nothing less than fine reading excites your palate.

The surprising part to all this is that it's more *fun* to read quality writing than hack writing. Once you develop a relish for the craft of writing, nothing else satisfies. Bubble gum writing quickly evaporates.

One thing that happens to literate college students is that they "discover" an author; they read everything the writer wrote, and force their friends to do the same. In my own college days before the Civil War, the favorites included Herman Hesse, Henry Miller, and Kurt Vonnegut; and then as now, many freshmen began their Ayn Rand phase. Your love of your author eventually dwindles, as will the other loves of your life, but you will have discovered literary passion and that endures forever.

You don't need to major in English to read; you only need a desire not to spend your life brain-dead. If you are majoring in a subject leading to a B.S. degree, and you value your spirit, read.

On Learning about the World: Nonfiction

For getting smart, magazines are better than newspapers are better than TV news . . . and books are better than magazines.

Start developing your own educational track that runs alongside your school track. Pursue your own private interests, your own special investigations.

Critics complain that the modern world is overly specialized and split into "Two Cultures," composed of literary types on the one hand and scientists on the other. If you want to get educated—and A's—learn to feel at home in both worlds.

Read popular science—especially if you are a non-science major.

Do you know a black hole from a quark? The current status of recombinant DNA? Superconductivity? You cannot consider yourself a well-informed adult in the twenty-first century if you are ignorant of scientific developments. Excellent books in every area of science have been written for the educated nonscientist, and you should read some of them.

Read biographies—especially if you are a science major.

Nonfiction cuts an enormous sweep of territory but I want to extol, in particular, the virtue of reading biographies. In college, you need a steady dosage of inspiration; for that you need to read biographies.

Biographies teach about specialness, which is why they won't write a biography of the insurance salesman down the block. Nice guy, decent life, but nothing about him cries out to be inscribed for posterity. Biographies are written about the extraordinary, about people whose lives made a difference.

Read biographies about those you admire—we all could use heroes—and those you despise. You need the infatuation, or conversely, the anger, to get involved in their lives. You'll come away with a deeper appreciation of history, psychology, determination, and luck.

THE BOOB TUBE AND YOU

According to a recent Carnegie Foundation study, 22 percent of college students spend more than nine hours a week watching television. I'm well aware of all the wonderful programs on public television and I'm also aware that these are not the programs you spend your time watching.

If you are hooked on TV, unhook yourself; you simply cannot afford to waste the time. Before long, you will miss television not at all and delight at how much more time you have for other activities.

Watch television only when you have nothing better to do. And you should almost always have something better to do.

THE LIBRARY

Here is where I get to rap rhapsodic.

The library is the scholar's sacred retreat, his temple of learning. Here the student of today converses with the sages of the past, and losing himself in their accomplishments, discovers the promise of his own.

Thank you. Now get your butt over there.

Until now the library's main function in your life was to serve as an alibi for when you were supposedly somewhere else. "I was at the library" was your standard excuse to your frantic parents, with "the phone wasn't working there" added when the questioning got intense.

A college library is more fully stocked than your neighborhood library, and you can turn to it as a permanent resource for filling gaps in your education. Suppose you need a refresher course in algebra, or your geographical picture of Asia is hazy, or you can't remember why Erasmus is important. The answer awaits you at the library.

That's not all. Are you thinking of buying a new car? Want to improve your racquetball serve? Planning a trip to Spain? Interested in magic, maps, migraine headaches,

Mongolian cooking, or mysteries? The information is at your college library.

You would think that college students spend much of their time in the library and don't need this prodding. You would think wrong. According to a Carnegie Foundation study, 65 percent of undergraduates are in the library less than four hours a week, 50 percent spend no more than two hours a week in the library, and one out of four undergraduates spend no time at all in the library.

If you want to ace college, you must turn the library into your home away from home. Join the tour of the library most colleges offer during orientation week, but return for a more thorough visit later when you're alone. Get a sense of the place: check out the stacks, browse about the reference section, survey the study lounges. If you're serious about your education, you will be camping out here much of your time.

The library is also a low-key, natural environment for meeting other students. No longer will you use the library as an alibi for your amorous rendezvous elsewhere—many a rendezvous begins at the library watercooler.

WHAT'S HAPPENING TODAY?

Go over to the bulletin board at the student building and read the fliers. Skip the notices of bikes for sale, shared-expense trips to Chicago, and proclamations to save the earth, and look for announcements of upcoming events. Even small colleges offer a supermarket of lectures, concerts, art exhibitions, theater, and films. If you aren't interested in "recent American policy in Angola," you might prefer dropping in on a poetry reading, hearing a talk on the history of jazz, or catching an early Buñuel film that never plays at the local mall.

The college campus is an ongoing cultural resource that's right in your own backyard.

EXTRACURRICULAR ACTIVITIES

You've come to college not only for a "book" education, but for a social education as well. You deprive yourself of a wholesome college life by locking yourself away in your room for the next four years. But this book isn't about improving your social skills, it's about improving your grades. The question here is not whether extracurricular activities will get you more dates (they probably will), but whether they will improve or hurt your grade point average.

The answer is—get ready for a big surprise—it depends. Much as with sex, drugs, and rock & roll, and everything else in life, it depends on what you do, with whom you do it, and how much. A recent study indicates that students who engage in intramural sports have better morale with no apparent decrease in grades. Joining the wrestling team won't hurt your grades, but it isn't likely to improve your grades either.

Academic Clubs

Academic clubs (clubs tied to a specific department) *can* have an appreciable and positive effect on your grades.

Consider joining a club affiliated with your major, especially in your junior and senior years. These clubs sponsor lectures, student debates, workshops, and tutoring jobs, while providing an opportunity to share ideas and gossip with like-minded students.

There are more calculating reasons for joining these clubs. Usually the chairperson of the department and the department faculty advisor are on close terms with the club members, particularly officers of the club. You will find this connection very helpful when you need special favors and letters of recommendation. Furthermore, in the course of hanging out in the department lounge, gossiping with the friendlier professors and the all-important department secretary, you will hear much useful inside information on the department politics. You will learn which professors have the real power, which have reputations for good teaching, which are the terrible graders, who will teach what next term, and who won't be teaching at all.

Give some thought to joining the academic club of a subject you are considering as a major. This is a good way to find out firsthand about the department, its faculty, the kind of students who major in the subject, and whether the whole package interests you. In fact, joining an academic club in a department other than your major is an excellent way to broaden your intellectual horizons.

Between sports teams and academic clubs lies the broad category of activities based on interests. The payoff for better grades is only indirect, but the payoff of involvement in an activity you care about is highly rewarding.

Do you enjoy writing or think you might? Work for the school newspaper or student literary magazine. Dream of a career as radio disc jockey? Spin records at the college radio station. See yourself as another Jack Nicholson or Meryl Streep? Strut your stuff in the drama club. Never again will you have available to you as wide a range of opportunities.

THE TRENDY AND THE
AVANT-GARDE

No matter what subject appeals to your interest, you must appreciate the difference between the trendy and the avant-garde. Most people are trendy about most things and a few are avant-garde about a few things. It works this way: The avant-garde are pioneers, leading the herd. The reward for pioneering is that you are among the first to witness the newest successes and, on occasion, observe the successes of tomorrow. The bad part is that more often than not you are the first to observe the dismal failures. In every human enterprise, junk always outnumbers quality; Burger King always has a bigger crowd than the fine French restaurant two blocks away.

Why bother? Because the few winners make the quest worthwhile. You partake in the formative stages of creative ideas, watch as movements emerge, and peek into your culture's future. Of perhaps even greater satisfaction, you belong to a community of the devoted few who share your devotion. That alone is worth the price of admission.

Suppose you are among the avant-garde with regard to the world of cinema. Unlike your college-mates who only see Hollywood movies, you are out there investigating the latest independent film, obscure documentary, foreign release. Most of what you'll see will never make the big time and for good reason: most new productions are somewhere between failures and utter disasters. But when one of these backwater movies does become successful, you can proudly proclaim that you saw the film back when the audience numbered fewer than twelve. It's much the same for the avant-garde in fashion, high-tech gadgets, vacation resorts, theater, music, sports, art, and the rest of civilization.

The hard-core trendy, a wholly other breed, aren't avant-garde about anything. Because they have no passion, they take no risks. Their restaurants have just been reviewed in trendy magazines and are populated with other trendy patrons. Ask them what they know about opera and they'll mention Pavarotti and change the subject. Talk about ballet and they'll talk about Baryshnikov and that is all. They read only best sellers. They listen only to top ten music hits. Particularly infuriating—and if you haven't met this trendy group, you will soon notice them sprouting all over your campus—are the political trendy who are forever aroused by the issue of the day: ecology, nuclear power, South America, and the Middle East one year, South Africa, AIDS, and the homeless the next year . . . whatever the current political fashion dictates.

Since you don't have boundless interests, boundless energy, boundless time, and boundless resources, you have to be selective about your avant-garde pursuits. Don't expect to be in the forefront of more than one or two areas. As for the rest, settle back with the crowd. If you are in the avant-garde about literature, say, you will read books that others do not, but you might be listening to the same music as all the other unenlightened peasants.

The benefits of belonging to the avant-garde in your college studies are far-reaching.

- You will find a faculty member who shares your interest and the professor–student imbalance will fade. You will be taken more seriously, and your discussions will become more conversation and less lecture.
- You will make important off-campus contacts. People with the same avant-garde pursuit are a community-at-large. This network will bring additional people into your

life, people on whom you can call after you graduate and enter the work force.

• You will experience scholarship for its own sake. You read, watch, listen, not because it will be on an exam, but because *you* want to know. Belonging to the avant-garde breaks down the artificial boundary between school and life.

The one essential condition for belonging to the avant-garde is that you genuinely care about the subject. If you aren't sincerely enthusiastic, interest will quickly fade and your taste will atrophy.

What creative area ignites your passion and sustains your dedication? The subject need not belong to "high culture"—you can participate in the leading edge of new Italian cooking, old comic books, Scrabble, or model airplanes; it's the commitment that counts. Decide where your interest thrives, step away from the masses, and move up to the avant-garde.

GETTING PERSPECTIVE

What is it like living one's life as a Buddhist monk?

What do you dream about when you are a member of a primitive society that believes they are the only human beings in the world?

What are your expectations when your father is emperor? A slave?

Climbing into Another's Skin

Getting educated is getting perspective. A wider view of issues directly improves your grades in the social sciences or humanities. Professors award high points to papers and essays that demonstrate an ability to see matters from another point of view.

We know a great deal about the people in our lives. The most immediate way of gaining insight into another person is by direct observation. You look, you watch, you note actions and reactions, and you infer how these other people feel on the inside.

But these inferences are limited. The imaginative leap into another's emotional state is always difficult, but even more difficult is climbing into another's philosophical skin. Different beliefs entail different lives. On the outside this difference is not always apparent, but inside, where life is experienced, the differences are enormous. Other people have different fears, different joys, different aspirations, different disappointments.

If you are intellectually curious, you will want to explore other beliefs. It's not a matter of judging the truth or falsity of these other beliefs, though you must eventually do that, too; nor is it about learning tolerance, though this is an inevitable consequence. It is about trying to "experience" without prejudice a view that differs from your own. This is true learning.

In this spirit, study other religions and atheism. Consider how other people regard work, sex, individualism, community, child rearing, tradition. Read other cultures' history and literature, listen to their music.

Many of you physically left your hometown to go to college. Leave your college town—intellectually—and tour the world.

Friendships

One way of expanding your perspective is by expanding your friendships.

In high school, you felt most comfortable with those who

shared your likes and dislikes, beliefs and disbeliefs. In college, you want to invite different kinds of people into your life. These friendships are extremely important. The longest lasting friendships are made in childhood and in college.

Make sure that at least a few of your friends are productive people; you want some of the passion of passionate people to rub off on you. You need that energy to excel in college.

You also want friends with varied interests; the best way to learn anything is to have a friend who lives the subject. You are interested in your friend's life, so you are interested in his interests; by osmosis, you will learn about your friend's specialty. Your inventory of knowledge will increase dramatically as a result . . . and your grades will improve as well.

I do want to caution you about one species of friend that can eat away at your own productivity: people who denigrate your enthusiasm. College is a time for many bursts of ideas, and you need people who encourage you. Don't become a victim of those who cannot share your exuberance.

You have this wonderful idea, and, excitedly, you describe it to your friend. A half an hour later, you walk away completely dulled and only vaguely know why. Your friend liked the idea all right but somehow managed to kill your enthusiasm. It's the way he liked your idea that's the problem—flatly and matter-of-factly. You are explaining your term paper project and just at the critical juncture your friend asks you for the time, or asks, by the way, how your brother is doing, or reminds you how nothing came of your last project, followed by the mandatory "Sorry, for the interruption, please go on." Yeah, sure. Eventually, you realize that something like this happens every time you try to share your ideas with this person.

This world is populated with wet blankets. They'll burden every new insight with a thousand criticisms, suck the juice from every spontaneous decision, deaden every joke. These individuals are insidious because they don't mean to harm you. They are, after all, your friends; they might even include someone you love.

Go on loving them—just take your ideas someplace else.

Cultivate friendships with foreign students. Thrust into a strange country, with only a minimal understanding of the local language and customs, foreign students deeply appreciate your friendship and companionship. These friendships will serve you at least as well. Through the course of these associations you discover details about your friend's culture that you would never learn just by reading books.

For much the same reason, cultivate friendships with people of different ethnic and social backgrounds. You learn from these friendships—in practice not theory—the virtue of tolerance, the stupidity of ethnic chauvinism, and how to see your own life from a different angle.

These friendships will improve your grades directly: you will know a lot more about history, geography, comparative religion, sociology, and much more. But you will also gain *wisdom*, and that deeper understanding of the world appreciably improves the way you approach your studies.

Travel

If the foreign culture won't come to you, go to it. Most colleges arrange for a term abroad, and I know of no college students who haven't found these semesters abroad rewarding . . . and lots of fun.

If you're creative, you can travel without spending a

great deal of money. I'm not talking about taking a luxury vacation on the Riviera (may you have many of those too) but of expeditions that are more adventurous and instructive.

Go someplace unfamiliar, someplace where people act in unaccustomed ways. A place where your only resource is your own resourcefulness.

To get along there, you will need to pay close attention to your surroundings and, in the process, you absorb a great deal of new information. Trips of this sort put in context much of what you study in history, political science, and languages. You learn a great deal about the world and even more about yourself.

KEEP A JOURNAL

College graduation day will be a sad day if you leave school with the same beliefs with which you began. You will have done college well, on the other hand, if your convictions about culture, politics, people, romance (the whole works) underwent change and development.

Schoolwork, your outside reading, friends, travels, joining the avant-garde, and your independent ideas will transform your beliefs and ideas.

Chronicle those transformations.

Keep a journal of your thoughts and other people's thoughts that provoke your own. Don't confuse this journal with the diary you kept for three weeks in junior high school—this isn't a log of your dentist appointments or about how upset you are with Macey for telling Stacey about Tracey. The point of *this* journal is to pay as close attention to your mental life as you do to your social calendar.

An "intellectual" journal prods you to formulate your thoughts, but since you can't formulate thoughts without having them, a journal also prods you to think. Your ideas will surprise you, and surprise you even more years later . . . "I believed this?!" Old convictions are as startling as old pictures (and sometimes as embarrassing).

What sorts of ideas go into your journal? Observations about people and your reactions to them, ruminations about God and the universe, reflections on books and movies, friends and adventures, choice quotes and phrases, fantasies and nightmares. It is a private forum for ideas and thoughts that matter to you.

This journal will accompany you beyond college, but while in school it provides an extra benefit: better grades.

Researching which bike to buy is work, but it's work you do well when you want to buy a bike; you read the relevant information carefully and check all your sources. If you have that attitude toward your schoolwork, you'll ace your classes. The need to personalize your school subjects and make them matter to you has been applied to various contexts: your term papers, the way you study for exams, talk to your professors, and, as just discussed, in elevating yourself from the trendy to the avant-garde.

A journal of your ideas helps bridge the gap between the ideas you study and the ideas you generate yourself. They become part of your ongoing education. As a bonus, a journal provides practice in transforming ideas into words—a very useful skill in writing essay exams and papers.

Buy yourself a fine notebook for this purpose since it will be your companion for many years. Make sure to date your entries (you won't write every day and you won't remember when you wrote what). You can, in fact, expect long periods of slack. Write when you have something to say.*

Keeping a journal of your ideas means taking your mind, beliefs, and ideas seriously. This is the central tenet of becoming educated.

*I do, however, want to warn you about brooding. College diaries are often morose diaries. Students write when swept into depression over lost love or no love at all, parental pressure, test pressure, or another of the thousand cataclysms that can ruin your day. If writing eases your pain, write. But remember, not all music is sad, not all paintings sullen, not all conversations grim; so write, too, when you feel joyous. Don't confuse brooding with serious thinking.

10

Cheating

Conscience is that small voice that makes you feel
even smaller.

We are never so easily deceived as when we imagine we are deceiving others.
— FRANÇOIS DUC DE LA ROCHEFOUCAULD

A friend of mine teaches political science at one of the city
of New York's college campuses. One day he received a
term paper that he read with increasing incredulity. At
first the paper seemed vaguely familiar, but as he read
on, the familiarity became vivid. *Why does this seem so
recognizable?* he wondered. It finally hit him—it was his
own paper!

This professor, it seems, had written that very paper
when he was a student. He passed it on to some other
student who passed it on to still another student, and so
on down the years. And here it was, back in the hands of
its original author.

My friend returned the paper with the following note:
"This is *my* paper. It received a B− when I submitted it
to my political science professor years ago. I thought then
that this was an unfair grade and I still do. So I'm delighted

to rectify the unfair grade and give the paper the A it justly deserves."

College students cheat. A lot.

Some cheat often, deliberately, and stupidly. Others cheat occasionally, reluctantly, and ingeniously. The methods and skill might vary, but the fact remains: college students cheat a great deal. Some surveys indicate that a clear majority of students have resorted to cheating while in college.

Now, of course, you are one of the honest minority. You say, "I didn't cheat in high school, and I won't start in college." Or perhaps you say, "Yes, I cheated a bit in high school, but now that I'm in college, no way." Congratulations on your integrity. But expect to have your resolve sorely tested.

First, you need the grade to get: (a) on the dean's list; (b) into law school; (c) off probation; (d) Dad to buy you the Camaro. Second, you had to stay home with your kid brother and couldn't get any studying done. Or maybe your roommate's pet monkey ate your notebook . . . anyway it's not your fault. Third, the teacher is a dud and deserves it. Fourth, this is chemistry, you're majoring in music, and you don't care about the subject. Fifth, this is chemistry, you're a chemistry major, and you need to do well in your major.

Sixth—and this is the most common reason for cheating—everyone else is doing it. Grades are competitive, you rightly argue, and if others are benefitting by illicit means, you'd be foolish not to do the same. It's as if you were playing a tennis match where only you were called for faults.

This is a serious and compelling argument. The answer, "Two wrongs don't make a right," begs the question: Why isn't it right to cheat if others, your competitors in a sense, are doing the same?

GETTING CAUGHT

One common—and inadequate—reason not to cheat is that you might get caught.

The immediate problem with this reason is that it's false! Unless you're a complete hog and very amateurish, you are not likely to get caught. Criminals who are apprehended are double losers (they can't make it in the straight world and they're failures as criminals). Most students who cheat, like most criminals, get away with it.

Let's be clear, though, that many *are* apprehended and you might be among them. While the main reason for not cheating has to do with the act of cheating itself and not with getting caught, the risks should not be discounted. The repercussions of getting caught can be extremely serious: failing the course is the best you can hope for, and suspension is not uncommon. So a few words about the hazards are in order.

Plagiarism

The riskiest form of cheating is plagiarism. Because plagiarism takes place at home or in library stacks, students think their cheating will go undetected. In fact, it's pretty easy to tell when a student has plagiarized.

The dumbest case of plagiarism that crossed my desk was in my philosophy of sports class. This course usually attracted some of the swiftest legs on campus, but rarely the swiftest minds. This particular student, though, was a classic.

The paper he submitted was a word-for-word copy of a chapter in the textbook we used in class. "For goodness sake," I asked with genuine wonder when I met with the student, "if you're going to plagiarize, at least go to the trouble of copying from an obscure book in the library.

Why copy the class textbook?" The fellow answered, "Look, I read the book and I agreed with the author. But he made the point much better than me, so I used his words."

Plagiarists always run the risk of getting caught. Unless you're an expert in the subject, you can't evaluate whether the material you are lifting is appropriate. You might be copying from a far-out source, obviously unprofessional or eccentric (obvious to your teacher, not you), or you might be cribbing from a source that's very well known to scholars in the area—and your professor.

Plagiarists give themselves away in hundreds of little ways. Invariably, they drop some word, phrase, or jargon used only by professionals in the field. When they discuss their paper with their professor later, it becomes unmistakable that they are faking it.

Students accused of plagiarism always insist that they just "summarized" someone's idea. At what point does summary become copying? How about if you "borrow" just a sentence? A paragraph?

As copyright lawyers who deal with similar problems in the law will tell you, no one can draw a precise boundary between extracting from another's work and stealing it. But you can determine whether you're plagiarizing or rephrasing someone else's ideas by reminding yourself of the purpose of writing a paper.

You are expected to read other sources (a research paper isn't an autobiography) and expected to make reference to those sources. But your central task is to present your *own* critical analysis *based* on your research. A plagiarized paper doesn't meet this aim. Placing quotes around the text helps you escape a charge of stealing, but not the charge of not having done your own work.

Most students have a pretty good idea whether their work is their own. Students copy from others not because they misunderstand the nature of plagiarism but because they are lazy or insecure about their own work.

THOSE CHEATING EYES

You can rob a safe by picking the lock or by blowing it up. You can invent a microwalkie-talkie earphone system that relates the right answers to you, steal a copy of the exam, or resort to the most basic cheating method of all—sneaking a look at the paper next to you.

Stealing a glance is a charge that is hard to establish, and even harder to deny. If your professor claims to have caught you looking at another student's paper, and you claim you didn't, you are *ipso facto* claiming that your professor is lying. So now you are doubly on the outs: one, you stand accused of cheating, and two, you have called your professor a liar.

Frankly, I think it's rare for a student to be unjustly accused of cheating. Professors are embarrassed by cheating; it means ugly recriminations as well as meetings with the chairperson and the dean. It's a royal pain that most teachers would rather avoid. I'm sure, though, that students have been unjustly accused and in those circumstances have no choice but to insist on their innocence. Just beware: it's your professor who issues the grade, and if he thinks you cheated, you're in deep trouble. Don't even look like you might be looking at another's paper.

THE REAL REASON NOT TO CHEAT:
IT'S WRONG

The main reason for not cheating is that it's wrong. A closely related second reason is that it does bad things to your self-respect.

Both answers might seem utterly obvious and utterly unpersuasive. They are neither.

I sometimes question my students about their attitude toward money. I'll make an offer: "For a hundred bucks, and a guarantee that you won't get into trouble, would you go next door, say 'Excuse me' to the professor teaching the class, get down on the floor, and lick his boots?" Sometimes I'll make a different offer: "For a thousand bucks, and a guarantee that you won't get into trouble, would you break the arm of that young lady sitting on the other side of the room?" Sometimes the responses scare the hell out of me.

Whoever said crime doesn't pay had to be kidding. Crime does pay, and often very well. It's getting caught that doesn't pay. More importantly, this is a strange notion— we should be honest because it's a profitable financial tactic?! The fact is, especially in the short run, honesty often results in a loss of money.

Every other day this van parks on my corner. In the open trunk are tools for sale at half the price of similar tools in the hardware store a hundred feet up the block. We all know how the van owner gets these tools. It's a secret all over the block.

Am I foolish for not buying a new wrench? You can develop all kinds of rationalizations for justifying the purchase and so can I. But I don't. I'm not being saintly; it's just that it's wrong to buy stolen goods and that is a good enough reason for not participating in the scheme.

It might sound simplistic, but the reason to be honest is because it's right to be honest and (exceptions aside) wrong to lie and cheat.

CHEATING DOES BAD THINGS TO YOUR SELF-RESPECT

One of my relatives—let's call him Jonathan—is a partner in a prestigious law firm. He makes, I figure, at least $200,000 a year. He has a problem, though.

Some fifteen years ago, he asked a friend of mine to take the LSAT exam for him. My friend Sam is very, very smart but not very, very ethical. He is now a hotshot scientist, but back then he took exams for hire. Jonathan was hoping to get into Harvard Law School and was leaning on his respectable 3.6 index. He had taken the law boards and did no better than average. So he called on Sam for help. Sam took the test for him and had an outstanding day, achieving a near-perfect score.

Jonathan got into Harvard Law School. He didn't make *Law Review*, but he did okay, and now he works with a reputable Wall Street law firm.

When I see Jonathan, we don't talk about it. I know he cheated, he knows I know, and he also knows that I know he knows I know.

And I keep wondering, *Does Jonathan think it was worth it?* Does he spend his life feeling at least a bit like a fraud? Can he ever relax, even on his ski trips to Vail?

How would you feel about yourself if you reached a successful position in your field through cheating? Would the money make it all right? These aren't rhetorical questions; they speak directly to your sense of personal worth.

You say, "Hey, I'll only cheat in college, and then it's over." To which I say, "Baloney."

College is the easy part. If you cheat in college, why shouldn't you cheat in business school, or law school or graduate school? "Okay," you say, "I'll cheat a bit in school to help me land the fine job, and then it's straight work thereafter." To which I say, "Double baloney." The opportunity to cheat, and the corresponding temptation, are all over the work place . . . any work place. Why think you'll cheat only in school and not later at work when the rewards for cheating at work are so much more immediate and substantial?

The question is not only *what* goals do you want to achieve but *how* do you want to achieve those goals?

Suppose you are playing one-on-one basketball and your opponent forgets the score and grants you one point more than you deserve. Would you ignore his mistake and take the point? Suppose that in a chess game your opponent accidently replaces a knocked-over pawn in the wrong square to his disadvantage. Would you fail to mention it?

It's absurd to win at chess or basketball by cheating. It negates the whole point of playing the game. Victory is only satisfying when it results from your skills. You can't be proud of your grades if they aren't *your* grades. If you respect yourself, you will take what you deserve, for better or worse.

A POSTSCRIPT

I recently spoke to my friend, the political science professor whose paper was copied by his student. Someone had told me a similar story and I wanted to know if my friend was telling the truth or just applying to himself a popular anecdote.

"Absolutely the truth," my friend insisted. "Though not the whole truth," he added quietly. He paused, and I nudged him to tell me all. "Well," he continued, "after all these years I've an admission to make. The paper that the student copied *was* the paper I submitted as an undergraduate. But I never really wrote that paper. . . . I too copied it from someone else."

11

Screwing Up

(From "Dejection: An Ode")
A grief without a pang, a void, dark, and drear
A stifled, drowsy, unimpassioned grief
Which finds no natural outlet, no relief
In word, or sigh, or tear—

—COLERIDGE

Adversity introduces a man to himself.

Unless you are inordinately smart and inordinately lucky, you won't get an A in every class you take. Whether it's a B for the A student, or a D for the C student, getting a substandard grade hurts. The important question is how you deal with that disappointment, and how you deal with it depends on whether or not you deserved the grade.

JUST DESSERTS

You Didn't Get What You Deserve

You are outraged. You confidently gave your professor a self-addressed card to mail your grade and expectantly awaited the morning delivery. The situation looked good: You had an A− on your midterm, an A− on your paper, your classwork was exemplary, you're sure you did well on the final, and you even gave your professor a lift to the station when his car broke down. So why are you staring at a postcard that says your grade for the term is a B−?

Professors sometimes give students lower grades than they deserve; this is true. But it is also true (and far more common) for professors to give students higher grades than they deserve; overgrading is rampant, undergrading is not.

Nice to know, you admit, but you are, nevertheless, teed off. The immediate problem is not professional grading patterns, but the B− in your hand, which should have been an A−. What now?

The best possible scenario is that your professor really meant to give you the A− but his pen slipped or the registrar was drunk when she recorded your grade. It might take some bureaucratic maneuvering, but you should succeed in getting the grade changed.

The more probable explanation for your poor grade is less appealing. Your professor says that he gave you the lower grade because you "blew the final" or because your classwork was less than outstanding. That's your professor's opinion, not yours. Your opinion is that your professor is a creep to the marrow of his bones.

You believe you were chiselled out of the grade you deserved and you are angry. You spend a few days entertaining yourself with daydreams of your professor on the rack of inquisitional tortures, boiling water cascading down his gnarled legs, fires at his chest, tigers gnawing at his face. More kindly, you just hope a pigeon mistakes him for a statue and does its thing on his head.

Indulge your fantasies and then let them go. I assure

you again that though this time the cards went against you, over the long haul you will get more grades that are higher than you deserve than lower.

You Underperformed

Your professor isn't the only one to blame for your low grade; you might have something to do with it as well. This is more serious: if you are the problem then you must be the solution.

No doubt, you have a ready excuse. Let's see . . . you have a genetic disposition against calculus, you were stricken with a premature case of Alzheimer's disease that just happened to coincide with the two hours of your exam, the dog that ate your take-home midterm also swallowed your notes for dessert. When necessary, I'm sure you're even more imaginative.

Some—but not all—excuses are excusable. If you have a good reason for doing poorly then don't beat up on yourself; throw the bad grade in the hamper with your other bad luck stories. Usually, though, your excuses are clearly lame.

Owning Up

Suppose you acted badly toward a friend. Do you want him to rebuke you—exonerate you on the grounds that "you aren't all there, as anyone who met your parents would understand"? Do you prefer being held responsible for your actions or pitied?

Most of us accept responsibility even when the consequence is the ire of others.

Curiously, when it comes to judging other people we reverse directions and forget all about the importance of responsibility. With exceeding magnanimity we revert to psychologese: "You have to appreciate the woman's up-bringing," we explain. "She's incapable of making rational decisions. She doesn't mean to be malicious, she just can't help it." We have a ready stock of mitigating explanations.

We also dip into that bag of excuses to exempt our own foul-ups both to others and to ourselves. We don't consider ourselves "nutso" of course, but we do rationalize: I was too tired to study, I was in a bad mood, the teacher was the pits.

A rush to absolve people of misconduct undercuts their self-respect; likewise, we weaken our own self-respect when we effortlessly pardon ourselves. We don't blame babies and animals for the consequences of their misbe-havior because we don't consider them autonomous beings capable of deliberation. We do punish grown-ups.

People have a right to be held accountable. And so do you.

Notice, by the way, that you have no problem accepting responsibility when you get an A in your class. Own up to your rotten grades as well.

DAMAGE CONTROL

How Serious Is an Inferior Grade?

A knock on the door and in treks a student, her sad face buried in her chest. Why so upset? Well, it seems that Ms. Perfect A received a B in her speech class and thus the pale suicidal demeanor I see before me.

I'm sympathetic, of course. Not to her plight—one B hardly seems lamentable—but to her pain and to her val-ues which allow for nothing less than a flawless performance. "Pitchers lose no-hitters in the ninth inning," I say, trying to cheer her up. "Yes, but they get to try again. I can't," she answers. "I'm in the second half of my junior year and I've ruined my academic record."

How to console her? If only she would see the bigger picture and realize how silly this all is.

Surely a B for a straight-A student is no cause for mourning, but what about a D or F for the more typical student? How damaging is a bad grade? Not very damaging at all. Ten years from now you will not remember your grades in 90 percent of your classes (unless you indeed graduated with straight A's—I never heard of a straight-B student). *You won't remember, you won't care, and neither will anyone else.* Ten years from now no one will ask to see your college transcript and no will study it if they do.

The only time your transcript gets examined is when you apply for graduate school or professional school. The main interest of graduate school is your grade point average, not a specific grade in a specific course. Your grades in your major might get special attention (not even that in the case of law school) but not any particular class in your major.

Employers, generally, couldn't care less about your grade point average. In fact, unless you want to highlight your honors, don't even bother including your GPA on your resume; it looks amateurish.

Forget the miserable grade or two. They will fade with time. Even the F.

When a Poor Grade Matters

There are a few instances when bad grades *do* count.

Honors, such as Phi Beta Kappa or *summa cum laude*, are a valuable adornment to your diploma. The difference between an A and a B can mean a lot if it determines whether you qualify for these prestigious awards. A difference in a grade or two can also determine whether you receive a scholarship. On the other side of the grade scale, if you are on probation and need a C to remain in school, that C becomes Holy Grail.

Is there anything you can do to avoid the lower grade?

In these touch-and-go situations, drop the class if the prognosis for a good grade looks grim (in most schools you have a few weeks to withdraw from a class). If you get a C− or less on the first test, the chance of acing the class is paltry; even if your professor tells you that with hard work you can still get a high grade, don't count on it. Give special consideration to dropping troublesome classes in your major. If you can't afford the bum grade, bail out.

Another option offered in most colleges is Pass/Fail. If you opt for this choice, you only get credit for a pass and your transcript shows either a P or F. Here, too, you usually have time before exercising this option: If the course seems too rugged, consider the Pass/Fail option.

Pass/Fail, incidentally, is a wonderful way to take classes that seem intriguing but too difficult. The only courses that you should try to avoid taking Pass/Fail are those in your major.

What about Incompletes? Incompletes are granted to students who for good reasons cannot complete their coursework (and in many colleges, even not so good reasons are good enough). A certified flu on the day of the exam, say, will usually win you an I grade.

Ask for an I only in emergencies or when you are certain to do no better than a D. An I grade merely postpones the burden to next semester and the overload can spoil yet another term for you. If you are having difficulties in a class, try to rough it out rather than apply for an Incomplete. You stand a better chance of getting a decent grade now than later.

Screwing Up a Whole Term

Underperforming in a class or two isn't catastrophic, but what about students who underperform for a whole term or year?

A shabby term is obviously worse than a lone shabby grade, but neither matters in the larger scheme. With regard to your grades, the bottom line is your *total* grade point average and not any particular term. Again, once you are in graduate school or employed, the details of your college transcript will never make any difference.

Are poor grades in some terms more damaging than in others?

According to folklore, students have the hardest time right in the middle of school, in the second half of their sophomore year and the beginning of their junior year: sophomore slump or junior blues, some call it. (But as with so many other pieces of folk wisdom, no one bothers to produce evidence in its support.) If you are going to have a miserable term, it's probably the worst time of all.

Students sometimes begin college badly and then have three wonderful years. Sympathetic eyes will note the vast improvement and discount the slow start. Students sometimes end badly after three wonderful years and sympathetic eyes will discount the last term as restless *senioritis*. A midcollege dive, even if more common, is harder to justify.

That's how graduate schools might size up your substandard term, but how do you see it? Is there a problem here you need to face?

SOLUTIONS

You Don't Need to Graduate in Four Years

Maybe you need to slow down. In fact, the majority of today's college students do not graduate in four years; five to five and a half years is becoming the norm. The prime reason for this slower pace is economics (spreading out the cost of tuition over five years is less burdensome than shelling it out in four).

Spreading out your college years might make sense if you are having academic problems. Take a lighter load, mix in a few easy, "gut" classes, or take off a semester. This will not harm your academic record, but pushing yourself beyond your abilities will. This isn't a race: Get to the finish line at your own best pace.

Balancing Work and School

Thirty percent of all full-time students and eighty-four percent of all part-time students work. Many of these students suffer academically because of their jobs.

It's a complicated juggling act: you need the income, you need the study time, and you need to watch "The Honeymooners." Something has to give, and it probably won't be the TV.

Don't kid yourself about your ability to perform at your peak at both your job and college. If you are employed, you are competing with students who aren't employed, and no matter how smart you are, outside work takes its toll in hours and energy.

You have a choice: work less and live on less, or cut down on your schoolwork by taking fewer credits.

Personal Pressures

College can engender enormous stress and many students find it hard to cope. Poor grades result.

If you are feeling overwhelmed, check out the counselling services on campus—they are there to serve you.

If you think it's just a rough patch you're going through and need a little more time than usual, take a lighter load of classes, or easier classes for a semester. You can always reenter the fast track later.

If the problem is more serious, consider taking off for a semester. You might need a breather for a while. Remember, a stumble may prevent a fall.

Partying

If the problem is "too much partying," it's time for a little soul-searching. I don't want to play shrink, and I don't want to play preacher either, so I'll make this sermon very brief: I've seen too many good students get caught up in the partying cycle and ruin their academic careers. Get your priorities straightened out. Enough said.

Reconsider Your Major

One reason students underachieve in college is because they are stuck in a major they don't enjoy. Somehow, back in high school, Michael "decided" that he wanted to be an accountant and proclaimed his major during the first week of college. Although Michael hated accounting from the beginning, he thinks it's a sign of failure not to pursue his decision. No wonder he's doing so badly—you can't excel when you dislike what you're doing.

Most of my students know more about what they will

do the rest of their lives than I know about what I will do this weekend. Do you want to be an eighty-year-old who lived the life he or she did because of the hasty decision of a nineteen-year-old kid? Some consider this early sense of direction a sign of pragmatic maturity; I think it's sad, even frightening.

The pressure to declare a major early on in college is unfair and unwise. How are you supposed to know what you want to do with the rest of your life? Maybe you will fall in love with Greek classics, or botany, or anthropology. There are exceptions, such as the violin prodigy who knew at age seven that the instrument was her calling. If you are as confused about career choices as the rest, join the gang. Your uncertainty is a sign of mental health.

My advice is that you hold off declaring a major until you must. Think of college, certainly the first few terms, as a smorgasbord of different subjects, some to be tasted, some nibbled, and the choice ones gobbled.

Be leery, too, of the notion of "practicality" when it comes to choosing a major. Who can predict with certainty which skills will be "hot" six years from now when you enter the job market? In the past ten years, MBAs and law degrees went through sharp cycles of supply and demand, as did college teaching jobs and real estate brokers. Your best bet is to choose a major that meets these two requirements: you love the subject and you are good at it.

Is This the Right College for You?

You chose the college you now attend after long and agonizing deliberation—or you never had a moment's doubt. Either way, you might have made a mistake. It's not irreparable . . . you can transfer.

You chose a large college but would do better in a small

one, or vice versa. You chose an urban school but would flourish in a rural setting, or vice versa. You want a more vibrant, active social life, or a quieter one. A change is sometimes just what you need.

But I warn you: wherever you go, you take yourself with you. Your difficulties in school might well have more to do with you than with the school, and if so, changing schools isn't likely to solve the problem.

On the other hand, your college and you might be a genuine misfit. A transfer might be the cure.

Although transfers are fairly easy in undergraduate school, there are a few attendant problems you should consider:

- While all colleges accept transfer students (everyone wants your money), the better colleges will look carefully at your transcript, and poor grades can keep you out.
- You might lose credits. One way for a college to lord it over another is by refusing to grant credit for the work you did at the previous school. Sure *they* gave you an A, but that was in a Mickey Mouse class that *we* wouldn't even think of offering.
- The new school might turn out worse for you than the one you're in now.

Go Away, Please

Travel is a wonderful way to refresh yourself. Often, all you need to rekindle your interest in school (and your life) is a change of scenery.

See if you can join one of the many "terms abroad" currently available. We noted earlier that a term abroad can benefit your overall education. It can also serve as a welcome escape when you are in a rut.

Consider working abroad for a spell without any credit. Taking a term off to travel can invigorate your studies or waste your time . . . *make your decision carefully*.

ON NOT BEING AN A STUDENT

I wish I could promise that if you try hard, study diligently, laugh at your professors' jokes, do all the assignments, volunteer for the blood drive, follow all the tips in this book, in short, do all you are supposed to do, you will graduate with straight A's. It is likely that you will do well, but are you guaranteed straight A's? No. Not everyone in college can perch at the top of his or her class.

You've heard repeatedly, "If you try hard enough, you can succeed at anything." I hate to bear bad news, but that aphorism is just a myth and a dangerous one at that.

Not everybody can excel at everything and it's folly to suggest otherwise. If you are just starting violin lessons at the age of twenty, dream about your concert debut but don't rent a hall. It's pernicious to persuade a tone-deaf would-be singer that if only he works at it, he can have a golden career as an opera singer. (It's also unfair to the guy's neighbor.) Sure, you know a woman who started skiing at forty and now is a leading professional skier. And I know a man who was hit by lightning twice.

With younger people the issue is far more complicated. Talent can be latent and too many college students refrain from developing their abilities simply because they didn't exhibit an ability early on. On the other hand, it's just as misguided to insist that you will succeed in developing a skill when the aptitude is clearly absent. Why invite needless frustration?

There is a different aphorism, however, which is true:

It isn't being best that is important, it's being the best that you can be that is important. Most people are capable of learning how to sing, paint, play an instrument, or work a computer well enough to achieve great personal satisfaction. We won't win Nobel prizes in these pursuits, but we will enjoy ourselves. Isn't that enough?

If you work hard at your studies at college you'll do well. As important, you will have done what you could. What more can anyone ask for?

The Adult
Student

The closing years of life are like a masquerade
party when the masks are dropped.
—ARTHUR SCHOPENHAUER

The surest way to get nothing is to wait for everything.

Do professors expect more or less from adult students?

*Does it help or hurt to bring up your personal experiences
in class?*

*Are study groups better with other adult students or
younger ones?*

Welcome back to school. Take a deep breath and have a
look around. Check out your new classmates: computer
prodigies and premature alcoholics, preppies and punk-
sters, the polished and the primitive, the poised and the
pretentious.

You feel old, unsure, out of place, like an anorexic at a
sumo wrestler convention.

Returning to college is an act of courage for any adult

and for some it requires downright heroism. Why put yourself through this regimen? Why go through the trauma of studying, tests, and all that time spent away from the rest of your life?

So if no one else has yet toasted your bravery, let me be the first: Congratulations. You deserve it.

We professors are glad to have you in our classes. Adult students are highly motivated and among the best. *Adults are also among the most grade-conscious students.* That's not surprising. Older students are deeply anxious about whether they have what it takes to succeed in college.

Adults do well in college, but they would do even better if they weren't so insecure. They also need to free themselves of the self-defeating assumptions they've accumulated over the years.

THE PEP TALK

You Are Not Alone

More than thirty million American adults are presently enrolled in educational programs. These include classes in vocational schools, learning annexes, correspondence courses, and schools of continuing education. Adult students take a dizzying array of classes from Tantric massage and Balinese drumming to raising pet wolfs and yuppie yoga. More than five million adults are also enrolled in traditional community or four-year colleges, either as part-time or full-time students.

If you feel secure in numbers, you should be feeling pretty sure of yourself these days. In 1977, 49 percent of all Americans were over the age of thirty. By the year 2000, the percentage of Americans over thirty will rise to 58 percent. The largest percentage of population increase will be among those sixty-five and older. The baby boomers have come of age.

The dramatic increase in the number of adults in college is a result not only of a change in demography but also a change in culture. Women have careers. Midlife job shifts are socially acceptable. People have more disposable leisure time and are bored with mass entertainment.

These population figures might not make a difference to you but they matter a great deal to college administrators. Big bucks are involved. It's in the interest of the college administration to be nice to you because you represent a very deep pool of potential students. Keep this in mind as you make your way through your college career.

Why Are You Back in School?

Adults are in college for three basic reasons.

- **The career seeker.** The career seeker is back in school because of professional goals. She is considering a career change or needs the degree because her employer says she does. Perhaps she has decided to become a lawyer but must first complete her B.A. or maybe it's a real estate broker's license she's after.
- **The social seeker.** Adults in this category arrive at college because they are bored. They are bored with talking about furniture or the Dallas Cowboys, bored with their friends, and bored with themselves. Often, they are single and bored with the singles' social scene. College offers adults the possibility of a new set of friends, maybe even new romance.

  I've come to recognize that many of my students are at least as interested in each other as they are in hearing me lecture. As singles scenes go, adult educational programs are among the best. The pressure is off, and you don't have to be on—the classroom is a natural setting for meeting people.

- **The knowledge seeker.** "They go to college seeking knowledge." These adults are the intellectually curious. Don't be cynical. We make it so hard for people to say without embarrassment that they want to grow intellectually. We permit them to join programs to lose weight, get better at tennis, undergo psychoanalysis, but we lose patience when they say they just want to learn more. But hiding among us, and you might be one of them, are people who would rather exercise their brain than their fanny; they enjoy books more than soaps.

Most adults return to college for a combination of these reasons and you have your own complicated motives for returning to college. Whatever those reasons be, you are here now so let's get you out with a diploma draped in honors.

"I'm Terrible at Math" and Other Self-Fulfilling Prophecies

Negative self-fulfilling prophecies are the nastiest, sneakiest, most destructive attitudes confronting adult students.

Self-fulfilling prophecies are predictions that make themselves come true. They pose a treacherous trap because you don't even recognize you've been ensnared.

Self-fulfilling prophecies often come in the guise of labels. Convince a kid that he's a good-for-nothing delinquent and he will act like one. "I'm a good-for-nothing junior-criminal so I may as well commit good-for-nothing junior crimes." Adults, too, fulfill their self-described labels. Describe yourself as "incorrigibly sloppy," or "lousy at public speaking," or "terrible at carpentry," or "unable to balance a checkbook," and you go a long way to making

sure you stay that way. **Negative self-fulfilling prophecies can be disastrous in college.**

One of the most common and destructive self-fulfilling
prophecies is "I'm terrible at math."

Back in your early school days you had some trouble
with mathematics and "decided" that you weren't good at
it. Soon thereafter you broke out in a rash every time you
faced a problem involving numbers and, after a while, you
would avoid mathematical problems altogether. The result? You did become lousy at math.

*The crucial question is, what are you going to do about
it?* It's difficult enough to break this self-imposed limitation
on your skills when you enter college at eighteen, but it's
far more difficult to shake it when you're thirty, forty, or
older and you've already spent decades convincing yourself
that you are a moron at mathematics.

Let's agree that you do have limitations. On the basis
of your past difficulty, I predict that you will not win a
Nobel Prize in physics. Sorry. Some people are better than
others at math . . . and at languages, cooking, and flying
kites. But you don't need to be a math whiz to get through
college and, with the right attitude, you will get through
with flying colors.

Now is the time for a fresh start. *The math is the same,
but you aren't.*

I teach a course called symbolic logic, which utilizes
symbolic notation. As soon as I start writing P's and Q's
on the blackboard, I hear the moans and groans. Symbolic
logic reminds people of math, and math reminds them of
their lifelong incapacity. "No way," they assure me, "I
can't do this stuff." "The heck you can't," I reassure them.
"This isn't math, it's logic, a brand-new subject for you.
Think of it as a new kind of puzzle; relax and enjoy."

When these students stop seeing logic as another math
class they do very well. But symbolic logic really is a lot

like math. These students who breezed through my logic class could have triumphed just as easily in their math classes if only they hadn't presumed their failure.

That's mathematics, but the same is true with foreign languages, chemistry, or bowling. You will face subjects that gave you heartache in the past, and you won't conquer them now either if you walk in wearing a mental straitjacket. Start seeing your past difficulties as just that, *past* difficulties.

So much for the negative self-fulfilling prophecies. The flip side of all this is the wonderful effects that can be achieved by *positive* self-fulfilling prophecies.

Popular wisdom about "the power of positive thinking" makes a great deal of sense. Convince yourself that you're a natural at tennis and you'll be more inclined to learn the game. Successful artists, professionals, and business people believe that they are among the best at what they do. Old Henry Ford made the point felicitously: "There are two kinds of people in this world, those who say, 'I can,' and those who say, 'I can't.' And they are both right."

Do not confuse self-confidence with self-deception. If you want to do well, talk yourself up, but don't start believing that college will be a piece of cake. If you do, you will set yourself up for many an upset stomach.

It's Too Late to Learn Hindi

A sister problem to self-fulfilling prophecies is the "it's too late now" defense. All college students suffer from this, but adult students suffer the worst.

If you want to succeed in college, you must get excited about learning new skills.

"I always wanted to learn French, but I'm too old to start now. It's just too late," you insist with genuine dejection. With the same shrug you turn away from studying calculus, or acting, or Renaissance literature, or zoology.

Too old? Poppycock. Let's agree that the best time to begin any pursuit is fifteen years ago. But that's history. Is it too late to start today? Isn't that what you said five years ago? Had you begun those piano lessons then, you'd be an accomplished pianist now (perhaps no Philharmonic recitals, but you would impress your friends). You will kick yourself five years from now if once again you succumb to sheer laziness. "It's too late" was an excuse then and it's an excuse now.

Take computers, for example. In fact, take computers for a course. (You might not have a choice, since many colleges now require a minimum degree of computer literacy to graduate.) Computers loom as the biggest worry for most adult students. They recognize the power of computers but think it's a tool for the next generation. This is just fear masquerading as realism.

One aphorism warns that "All beginnings are difficult," and another reminds us that "A journey of a thousand miles begins with one step." Put on your walking shoes. Right now is a wonderful time to start learning computers or any other new field. It will take discipline and stamina and you won't taste the sweet rewards until you are well along, but hang in there, see it as a challenge, and you'll do just fine. I promise.

Have You Gotten Stupider?

For the second time this week you've forgotten where you put your keys. You are finding it harder to concentrate than you did when you were younger. "This just proves what I suspected all along," you conclude. "My memory is going and I'm just not as sharp anymore. I'm too old to be in school."

Hold on there, rusty old-timer. We aren't letting you off so easily.

Forget about the notion that your mental faculties significantly slow down when you get older. When you're *much* older, your short term memory might be affected. But numerous studies confirm that IQ loss is negligible even in old age and in many ways, the wisdom you've accumulated over the years makes you even more formidable intellectually.*

The deterioration of your body is another matter. Unless you've swigged from the fountain of youth, you are aging physically: your hair is thinning, your skin is wrinkling, your lung capacity is decreasing, your waist is widening, your muscles are weakening, and your teeth are loosening. Your entire body is shrinking, though your nose and ear lobes are growing. Mercy, enough. Anyway, none of this has any bearing on your schoolwork.

---

*Need role models? Try these:

· At the age of 89, Arthur Rubinstein performed one of his most memorable concerts at Carnegie Hall.

· At the age of 88, Michelangelo was deep at work on one of his great Pieta sculptures. (A few days before his death, he remarked, "I regret that I die just as I am beginning to learn the alphabet of my profession.")

· At the age of 87, George Burns gave a special command performance for the queen of England. (Someone commented that the only thing older than Burns were a few of his jokes.)

· While in their eighties, the American publisher Bernard Mac-Fadden parachuted into Paris and did a jig when he landed; Monet completed his most significant paintings; Manet too was painting industriously; Agatha Christie continued to write acclaimed mystery plays; Bill Kane won rodeo prizes and Levi Burlingham, a jockey, continued to win races; Benjamin Franklin helped frame the Constitution of the United States.

Your eyes and ears, however, do have much to do with your schoolwork. If you can't see what's written on the blackboard or read the small print in your text, take remedial action. Ophthalmologists recommend that you get your eyes checked regularly after the age of forty. Hearing loss doesn't become an issue for most people until much later, but Americans are suffering hearing loss at younger ages than ever before. The African bushman, living quietly in his noise-free environment, suffers no measurable hearing loss at age 60. By comparison, according to a study by the University of Tennessee's Noise Laboratory, 60 percent of American college students already suffer from high-frequency hearing loss. If you find yourself straining to hear your professor, get a hearing test.

Act Your Age

Check out that fifty-three-year-old woman dressed in the miniskirt with the blue hair streaked crimson and the "Rock & Roll Will Never Die" pin stuck on her sleeve. She's spirited and lively. She's also pathetic.

It's tough to act your age when it's twice that of everyone around you. It's especially tough in this country, which, despite its aging baby boomers, is still fixated on youth. When was the last time you saw a *Playboy* magazine centerfold with a woman in her forties? In her thirties? In the United States, it seems that over twenty-five is over the hill.

You *are* more mature than your classmates. You have more experience, and you have a broader perspective. You are, in fact, older. Get used to the idea and make it work for you.

PRACTICALITIES

My Son the Dentist

I think I can speak for most professors in saying that the worst feature of adult students is their proclivity to talk in class, without relevance, about their personal experiences. Too many adult students use class time to rehearse their memoirs.

We are in a child psychology class. Mrs. Goodson raises her hand.

"May I say something about that? When my son was little—he's now an orthodontist, by the way, and well known in his field—in fact, just three weeks ago he was invited to lecture in Tahiti—anyway, to get back to the point, when Dennis was three he used to get these terrible asthma attacks and what we'd do was this. We'd fill the tub with hot water—I remember many a night doing this at three in the morning—the idea was for Dennis to breathe in the steam. Dennis hated this, so his older brother Stuart—he's now in the insurance business. . . ."

Blah, blah, and more blah. A few students will find Mrs. Goodson's rendition "cute," and the professor might find it charming as well, but it won't help Mrs. Goodson's image as a serious student and it won't help her grade.

Speak up if your personal experience sheds light on the subject; a little applied reality helps anchor theoretical discussion. But don't use the class as an audience for your life story; if your personal history isn't relevant to the issue, keep it personal.

What? You People Don't Understand Price/Earnings Ratio?

"The kids today, they don't know anything." Adult students sometimes adopt this patronizing attitude toward their younger classmates, who reciprocate with unabashed disdain. Do you recall the anger you felt at nineteen toward older adults who offered their unsolicited advice on how to run your life? Mention your experience without dumping on everyone else. It's not smart to alienate your fellow students.

Conquering Pride: Teachers, Tutors, and Tears

You've taken your first test since being back in college and you got a C− or worse. Here was the first test of whether it made sense for you to return to school and you blew it. What do do?

Get some perspective. Your classmates have been taking classes and tests for the past twelve years, and they screw up too. It's only reasonable that college will take some getting used to.

Don't imagine that everyone is watching in judgment:

Rabbi Akiva was a poor shepherd who didn't begin his studies until the age of forty, and then went on to become the greatest scholar of his generation.

According to the legend, after Akiva married at the age of forty, his wife urged him to go to Jerusalem to commence his studies.

"I'm forty years old and know nothing," he said to her. "What will I achieve? Everyone will laugh at me."

His wife asked that he bring her a donkey. She then covered the donkey with herbs, dirt, and earth so that the donkey looked ridiculous.

The first day they brought the donkey to the marketplace everyone laughed at it. They laughed the second and third day as well. But then the oddity passed, and no one laughed any longer.

"Go and study," Akiva's wife told him. "Today they will laugh at you and tomorrow too, but the day after they will just say, 'That's Akiva, that's the way he is.' "

If you are embarrassed, you can't learn. Accept your bad grade for what it is—no more, no less. Then get some help. This isn't the time for foolish pride.

Tutors

Visit the department in the subject you need assistance in and ask for a tutor. Most departments have graduate students who are looking for tutorial work; often it is part of their scholarship obligations. The sessions are private, so you can ask the basic questions you are too embarrassed to ask in class. You go at your own pace and have the opportunity to concentrate on the problems that give you the most trouble.

Classmates

It's a good idea to review with your classmates before exams.

- Sometimes students are better at explaining than professors; they may better understand what is confusing you.
- You'll find out that you know as much as the other students. (Or, to put it another way, that they know as little as you do.) This can be very comforting.
- Usually, a few students are linked to the right network. They might have leads on the kind of exams the professor

likes to give. Even better, they might have copies of old exams.

Your Professor

Adult students and their professors have a special relationship. Often they are of the same generation and have a shared history. Most professors that I know will go that extra bit to help out adult students. Don't be shy about seeking it out. Get an appointment to meet during office hours and ask for help with your coursework.

The psychological tensions are sometimes trickier when your professor is considerably younger than you. Some junior professors feel awkward in a position of authority with someone older than themselves and some students have a hard time being judged by someone their junior. Just remember that your professor is a professional in his field only as you are an authority on the things you know best. You have no problem with having a doctor or accountant younger than you, and you're probably used to cops who seem to have started shaving just two weeks ago. College teachers like to portray themselves as experts on every subject imaginable—Lord help us if they are. Respect them for their knowledge, but don't defer to the authority of position.

Take It Easy

I can't say this too often so I'll say it one more time. Your performance in school is not a measure of your worth so don't make it that. It's great that you've decided to come back. Relax, study, and have a good time, and remember what Robert Frost said: "The reason worry kills more people than work is that more people worry than work."

What Matters: A Concluding Sermonette

A purple-eyed alien, complete with antennae and slimy skin, offers you a deal. You will graduate college with a 4.0 G.P.A., straight A's. He'll see to it, guaranteed. The trade-off is that you will learn *nothing* during the four years you spend in school. He will arrange it so that during tests—and only during tests—you know the answers to all the questions. He will provide you with term papers, untraceable, especially prepared for you on his planet, Shtooyoht. That's the deal: straight A's—but nothing learned in your four years of college.

Agree to the exchange?

If you answer yes, you are less likely to get A's in the real world. More important, if you answer yes, you need to rethink your priorities.

Students obsessed with A's tend not to get them. Certainly, A students care a great deal about their grades, and a few are among the obsessed. But, unlike other grade-conscious students, better students spend more time thinking about their studies than their grades.

This theme has been stressed throughout this book: if you don't care about what you're studying, you won't learn it. Only when you approach the subject as information *you* want to know will you make the effort necessary to ace the course. This isn't professorial cheerleading—it's the route to superior grades.

Taking your education seriously is the key to better grades, and we all agree that grades are important. But let's also be clear that grades are not—as the alien's bargain would otherwise suggest—more important than an education. Grades mark the *progress* of your academic education—they aren't the *purpose* of your education.

A thorough education is not only about assimilating the kind of information you can put to use on exams. It includes more than just nonacademic learning about the world. The education you are looking for also involves the development of your values and beliefs.

I don't know if it's a feature of age, environment, or a combination of both, but it is in college that we begin to reflect seriously on our lives. Everything is open to doubt and readjustment: our values, our convictions, our goals.

The turbulence can be wrenching or exhilarating, and much of the time it is both. For the first time, your choices have immediate and tangible consequences: "what matters?" matters. Based on your judgments, you decide on what subject to major in, how to spend your evenings out, and how to relate to your parents, friends, and lovers.

A change in "what matters" also entails a change in "who matters." You develop new idols. You fancy yourself a bohemian artist clothed in black and eccentricity; or you aspire to corporate power and act like the future tycoon; or you practice the roles of the bon vivant, the brilliant young scientist, the superstar athlete. Whom you choose as your role model helps mold your emerging adult personality.

Who you want to be depends on what matters to you; but what *does* count for you? Power? Money? Brains? Romance?

Sure, you want it all. But in what proportions? What is your hierarchy of importance? One person's "healthy balance" is another's fanaticism.

It's always difficult to know what really matters to you, but it's supremely difficult to get it straight when your values are in flux—as they are now or will be soon.

Part of us esteems certain qualities because we possess them ourselves: folks with talent admire talent, folks with money admire money, folks with good looks admire good looks. Conversely, a part of us admires those qualities that we don't possess: the drab envy the charming, the poor aspire to wealth, the homely dream of glamour.

The web of self-deception can be denser still. We sometimes convince ourselves that what we *wish* would matter to us *does* matter.

You get turned on by the idea of owning a stretch limo but you don't like the idea that you are materialistic. Appearances do matter to you, even though, if asked, you'd insist that a person's looks shouldn't figure in relationships and that your judgments aren't only skin deep. I know many college students who think they *ought* to love jazz so they convince themselves that they *do* love jazz, when, in fact, they never voluntarily listen to that music.

We lie to ourselves not only about our values but about our opinions.

You come to college with a set of beliefs neatly packed in your luggage. You have convictions about the big questions of God, religion, politics, sexual morality, and the major issues of the day, from abortion to the ozone layer. It isn't always clear how you got these opinions, but have them you do.

Until now your views had no teeth; they were just positions you rattled off when asked. Now they make a difference to how you live your life—and they are your responsibility. You must decide whether to pray and how, whether to have sex and with whom, whether to vote and for whom, which causes are worth demonstrating for, which worth demonstrating against, and which worth ignoring altogether. These are no longer debating-club issues to consider from a remove; the issues are immediate, and your responses define who you are.

The cafe and dorm room will become the laboratories for your ideas. Here, in the wee hours of the night, you discover how you think about these looming questions. And, incidentally, the skills of argumentation you develop in the course of these intense exchanges will show up to your benefit on your essays and in class discussions.

You will look back fondly at these intellectual intimacies. Most people are too intellectually tired to reconsider their beliefs; they interpret their laziness as "consistency" and make a virtue of it. One hopes you haven't yet been trapped by that inertia.

You will argue vehemently for your views, and it won't be easy to maintain your intellectual honesty along with your passion. We need to think especially clearly about issues we care about most, but it's precisely when we care a great deal that subjectivity overwhelms reasoning.

Maintaining intellectual honesty is especially difficult when we change our views. What seemed so right before now seems so wrong. Don't be surprised to occasionally find yourself hating what you once loved: think of the venom in so many divorces, the former smoker's crusade against smoking, or the zealous proselytizing of new religious converts. It's as if a negative sign were placed in front of our feelings: the stronger the previous attraction, the stronger the present revulsion.

Step back when you find yourself raving against a point of view that everyone else sees as no more than a minor irritation. Does the issue really deserve all this rancor? Are you being objective, or is it your past acting up?

How do you preserve your intellectual honesty within this swirl of changing ideas and values? How do you choose between the many often opposing views that come at you full force both in and out of school? I suggest that you keep the following two points in mind.

First, don't expect to work it all out.

Complicated issues are, by definition, unyielding to quick and easy solutions. People have a hard time with perplexity and opt for any answer that promises a solution. But getting the answer may not be as important as recognizing the depth of the problem and asking the right questions. Confusion is often a sign of mental health, so learn to live with it.

Second, keep your standards high. Don't undervalue your capabilities.

One of the most significant aspects of your college life is the chance it affords to work at full capacity. Let me tell you, this opportunity is rare.

Most people idle through most of their lives. There are exceptions, of course: the professional athlete, the driven research scientist, the dedicated doctor or lawyer, the prolific artist, and a few folks at top management. But how many people can honestly say that they can't do what they do any better than they're doing it now?

You can get away with underachieving in most of what you do—we underachieve as friends, lovers, children, parents, athletes. *But living and working below capacity is draining.* Hard work, on the other hand, as all exercisers know, leaves you winded in the short run but energized in the long run.

Back in high school you had a norm of expectations; you saw yourself as an excellent or fair student as the case may have been, and had a general sense of how hard you wanted to study. Now you're in college, and it's time to establish a new standard for yourself.

College students are easy prey to the temptations of underachievement. The distractions are varied, unending, and compelling, and it's easy to become cynical about your schoolwork. If you succumb, your four years of college will leave you knowing less than you should and with diminished self-esteem.

When, on the other hand, you take your complete education seriously, you begin to value your time; dull parties and Mickey Mouse classes leave you bored, as do your unimaginative friends and banal books. You also maintain high standards of evidence—the sloppy arguments that appeal to the masses are no longer good enough for you. These are *your* values and beliefs at stake—and you want to get it right.

Take yourself seriously, and the A's will come. Take yourself seriously and you'll ace it all.

FOR THE BEST IN PAPERBACKS, LOOK FOR THE

In every corner of the world, on every subject under the sun, Penguin represents quality and variety—the very best in publishing today.

For complete information about books available from Penguin—including Pelicans, Puffins, Peregrines, and Penguin Classics—and how to order them, write to us at the appropriate address below. Please note that for copyright reasons the selection of books varies from country to country.

In the United Kingdom: For a complete list of books available from Penguin in the U.K., please write to *Dept E.P., Penguin Books Ltd, Harmondsworth, Middlesex, UB7 0DA.*

In the United States: For a complete list of books available from Penguin in the U.S., please write to *Dept BA, Penguin,* Box 120, Bergenfield, New Jersey 07621-0120.

In Canada: For a complete list of books available from Penguin in Canada, please write to *Penguin Books Ltd, 2801 John Street, Markham, Ontario L3R 1B4.*

In Australia: For a complete list of books available from Penguin in Australia, please write to the *Marketing Department, Penguin Books Ltd, P.O. Box 257, Ringwood, Victoria 3134.*

In New Zealand: For a complete list of books available from Penguin in New Zealand, please write to the *Marketing Department, Penguin Books (NZ) Ltd, Private Bag, Takapuna, Auckland 9.*

In India: For a complete list of books available from Penguin, please write to *Penguin Overseas Ltd, 706 Eros Apartments, 56 Nehru Place, New Delhi, 110019.*

In Holland: For a complete list of books available from Penguin in Holland, please write to *Penguin Books Nederland B.V., Postbus 195, NL-1380AD Weesp, Netherlands.*

In Germany: For a complete list of books available from Penguin, please write to *Penguin Books Ltd, Friedrichstrasse 10-12, D-6000 Frankfurt Main I, Federal Republic of Germany.*

In Spain: For a complete list of books available from Penguin in Spain, please write to *Longman, Penguin España, Calle San Nicolas 15, E-28013 Madrid, Spain.*

In Japan: For a complete list of books available from Penguin in Japan, please write to *Longman Penguin Japan Co Ltd, Yamaguchi Building, 2-12-9 Kanda Jimbocho, Chiyoda-Ku, Tokyo 101, Japan.*